Crewkerne

and the Ham Stone Villages

IN OLD PHOTOGRAPHS

Bill Swaffield, who was to become one of the best-known men in the garage business in south-west Somerset, is pictured here at the entrance to the family business in East Street around the age of six in 1928. Hopefully the petrol (?) pump is not connected up. Note the old post office on the other side of the street which has now moved a few doors to the left to be nearer Market Square. The garage business is still run by the Swaffield family (see page 24).

Crewkerne

and the Ham Stone Villages

IN OLD PHOTOGRAPHS

Collected by GERALD GOSLING
and FRANK HUDDY

Alan Sutton Publishing Limited
Phoenix Mill · Far Thrupp
Stroud · Gloucestershire

First published 1993

British Library Cataloguing in
Publication Data

A catalogue record for this book is available from
the British Library.

Typeset in Sabon 9/10.
Typesetting and origination by
Alan Sutton Publishing Limited.
Printed in Great Britain by Redwood Books,
Trowbridge.

Crewkerne's Carnival Queen Lila Hunt, seated at the rear of the Queen's Float, immediately prior to the Afternoon Procession on 21 September 1935. There were always two processions, the afternoon one at 2.30p.m. for the children and an evening (6.00 or 7.00p.m.) one for the adults. In 1935, when the official opening in Market Square was performed by Lady Stavordale, Captain H. Hussey was chairman and Mr R.E. Comer and Mr B. Denman joint secretaries with a general committee that 'consisted of a large body of Ladies and Gentlemen of the Town and Country Districts'.

Contents

Crewkerne Volunteer Fire Brigade, 1902. The spotlessly turned out equipment and horses, not to mention the firemen, were housed in this courtyard which is now the site of Leo's Shop. On the extreme left is Jim Moerton, a carpenter from Belle View Terrace who had a workshop in West Street; others include Mr McCready the driver, Harry Wheadon and Jim Old. Crewkerne is said to be the first local town to have had its own fire brigade, records dating it to at least as far back as 1782 when the engine was housed in the Shambles. Details of expenditure on the brigade's equipment often can be found in the parish records, including, on 8 April 1787, 'George Holland's bill to reparing Engen Pype and 5 Pailes, taler (tallow) etc, 10s.6d. To 2 quarts of oil to oil the engine pipe, 1s.6d.; Paid Mr Dummett's bill to mending pump handle, 2s.6d. Paid to Ham Hill, stone used about putting up the pump in Hermitage Street left unpaid by Mr John Cox (churchwarden), 1s.9d.'

Things seemed to have deteriorated by the end of the nineteenth century because a public meeting was called 'for the purpose of establishing a fire brigade to work the parish fire engines'. Ratepayers had petitioned for the brigade after a vestry meeting had decided that the best of the two parish engines should be repaired as recommended by Shand Mason and Co., and that a new engine be bought at the expense of the parish. In September 1876 the new engine (probably the one in this picture) arrived; its first captain was Mr John Perry.

Introduction

Visiting Crewkerne in 1948 while on a cycling tour, I recall spotting the lovely castle-like, fifteenth-century parish church of St Bartholomew with the setting sun lighting up its golden stone. I came back again in 1960 while searching for a teaching post, reliving the past and remembering friendly people with old-time courtesy, girls with long hair and soft voices and a busy bustle all day long in the streets and shops.

Family shops were small and friendly in those days with a high standard of service and a chair to relax in while the shopkeeper ran around for you. At London House the grocer's assistant loved to hook down the packets high up on the shelves, and in West Street Mr McArthur at his art shop was the nicest man you could meet – he preferred to talk rather than sell. Bessie Dodge's trim shop in Abbey Street was tiny when filled with customers, but supplied fresh fruit and vegetables to a high standard. In Market Square there was Mr Hancock's drapers shop, dark downstairs with repairs kept to a minimum and spongy stairs which sagged at every step as you groped your way up them. Once safely upstairs one was amazed at the old-fashioned goods on display: iron-clad corsets, spencers, terrible felt hats and even a fox-fur stole. Oscar's Antiques was a red-gold wallpapered café with old settles and a real fire where home-cooked meals completed the picture. Two sisters kept the tea-shop in the Victoria Hall, now an electrical goods shop. One was Mrs Freeman, whose caged canary hung unhygenically over the tables, but there were home-made cakes and scones available all day and she proved to be a good friend to chat with. In an old listed Tudor house in South Street there was a hairdressers, complete with a barber's pole, where I had easily the best perm I have ever had; everyone was upset when the Council demolished the building without permission. I cannot end these reminiscences without a mention of Stan Wootton, the fishmonger in Market Square who regaled me with stories of his youth, including receiving the cane most days for being naughty in school. I miss his humour and simplicity. We are all the better for knowing these characters and I bless their memory.

It was some time before I cycled to see the quarry which provided the golden stone for so many buildings in the area. It is all hillocks and hollows where the Celts and Romans would have had the best views, the hill being higher then. We have the Beauchamp family to thank for the lovely priory at Stoke under Ham, now well looked after and with the pigeons returned, if not to the circular columbarium, at least to the adjoining barns. Here the Fleur-de-Lys Inn and its Fives Court still remain. The lovely Norman church with Sagittarius over the doorway and many Norman remains is also well worth a visit.

South Petherton, King Ina's Saxon village, has so much to commend it. The Daubeneys held the parish, as well as Barrington, for hundreds of years until 1543. Vicars since 1080 have embellished the church with its many coloured windows and monuments. Barrington with its winding street contains many good cottages and medieval farms still bearing the names of their early owners – Lye, Eason, Budd, Denman, Royce, and Brownsell. An unspoilt church and the Tudor Court at the eastern end complete the picture.

I can remember The George at Hinton before the fire; its wall seemed to curve round the corners, the thatch beautifully softening the buildings. My journey each day to Crewkerne took me through Misterton, a border village only just in Somerset where, with great artistry, one farmer finished a clamp of root crops with a roof of turves. Mr Holder could be seen and heard at work in his smithy near the centre of the village, where the road dips down to the inn. One can wander down the side lanes here to the church; this is near to where the novelist Helen Mathers wrote her books which included so many recognizably local scenes.

Shepton Beauchamp is a thriving place with much to see. Try to find the two medieval farms still there and see the old lanes, Robins, Love and Buttle, complete with their pretty gardens. St Michaels' thirteenth-century church, high on its mound, overlooks the village.

Some will say I have left the best to last. The golden Ham stone continues to please in the old town of Martock in a superb church with a timbered roof showing 750 panels, and an old manor house and school nearby.

I have great pleasure in introducing this book filled with remembrances; the past which it explores is both evocative and enduring.

Patricia Pearce, Shepton Beauchamp, 1993

SECTION ONE

Crewkerne - the Place

Barrett's first butchers shop in South Street, seen here decked out for Christmas 1888, the year the firm was first established. Poultry, which was still a luxury until mass production came along after the Second World War, is conspicuous by its almost complete absence here. Today the premises are Bryants bakers shop. Gaiters appear to have been part of a butcher's 'uniform' in these days. Later the firm moved to Market Street (see page 20).

The Parrett & Axe Vales Dairy Company, Hermitage Street, *c.* 1900. The collection carts, forerunners of today's pump-out tankers, covered the area from Beaminster almost to Yeovil, as the name Parrett and Axe Vales suggests, and, come sun, rain, snow or blizzard, made a daily collection. It must have been a tough job, especially to the south of Crewkerne where the ground falls steeply away towards Beaminster. The entire yard and the field in front with its handsome crop of potatoes has been the scene of the housing development which has steadily marched up Hermitage Street and Lyme Street.

Later, the Parrett & Axe Vales Dairy Company became The English Dairies Ltd, and here, around the outbreak of the First World War, deliveries have moved into the motor age. Compared with the picture above, the processing plant has had a face-lift and grown a chimney stack and, if compared with the picture opposite, an office block has been built to the left of the entrance and housing has appeared on the other side.

Agricultural shows are the dairy trade's shop window, and The English Dairies Ltd was no exception. This stand, thought to be at a Bath & West Show around 1912 hardly goes in for gimmickry in advertising, just piles of what the business was best at – Meadowvale Butter, Axe Valley Cream, and a genuine, and mouth-watering, Cheddar mountain. Note the jams and, presumably, honey at the rear.

The English Dairies Ltd, Hermitage Street, *c.* 1914.

The Open Air Swimming Baths, Viney Bridge, were opened in 1935 by Mr W. Taylor, the then Chairman of Crewkerne UDC; they are seen here soon afterwards. The baths developed a leak in 1952 and were closed, becoming the garage and yard of Crewkerne Road Transport. Today the area is scheduled for housing development.

Crewkerne station, seen here around 1899, was opened in 1865 on the old London &
South-West Railway Waterloo–Exeter line, and is actually in Misterton parish. The station
omnibus, most likely driven here by Eli Watts, was known as the 'sixpenny coach' because
that was the fare to carry passengers to the Red Lion or the George Hotel in the town
centre. Legend has it that the landlords of the two hotels mentioned above played a annual
game of dominoes to decide who would operate the coach for the next twelve months.

This National Bus in Crewkerne Square in 1921 was the first bus between the town and
Yeovil calling at West Coker, East Chinnock and Haslebury Plucknett. Monty Hopkins
was the driver, Emily Vile (on step) and Gertie Best the conductresses, one of them
obviously from another bus. The solid wheels could hardly have given a comfortable ride,
even along the then A30 trunk road to Yeovil from where the bus operated. It is worth
noting that no one had realized yet that a bus could be used as a mobile bill-board.

The Square, *c.* 1880. The Royal Field Artillery made an overnight stop at Crewkerne on its way to the Okehampton ranges. The guard-room was set up in the White Hart and a guard mounted over their field pieces which were parked in the square. The men were billeted in local pubs which presumably stabled the horses as well.

London House, *c.* 1932. Robert Gutsell's, a popular draper and sports outfitter, was an old-established shop which was to be demolished in 1961 to make way for a new block of shops with offices and flats above, but reprieved. Gutsell's, in common with most other shops in the town, always closed early on Carnival Procession Day (a Saturday) in order 'to allow the staff to be free'. The procession started at seven o'clock, and the shops closed at seven o'clock! Gutsell himself would have left earlier as he was on the Marshal's Committee during the 1930s.

Church Street, *c.* 1870. Apart from the shop windows, Church Street is little changed today. Note the drinking tap in front of the handsome gas lamp standard which was removed (unnecessarily as it happened) during road improvements.

East Street, 1868, looking towards Market Square. Most of the property on the right-hand side of the road at this point, including the area behind the railings, was, in later years, the offices and shop of the South Western Electricity Board.

Bradford & Sons, the Yeovil-based coal and general building merchants, had depots in many of the towns and villages in south-west Somerset, West Dorset and East Devon. Invariably, and for obvious reasons, these were always at railway stations as was, and still is, Crewkerne's which was built shortly after the London & South-West Railway's Waterloo–Exeter line reached the town in 1865.

The Viney Bridge area of Crewkerne on the Dorchester road was always prone to flooding, as this picture, dated December 1954, shows.

The old Crewkerne Hospital, South Street, *c.* 1900. The hospital was demolished around 1969 to make room for the entrance to the proposed South Street car park. The tall chimney was for the laundry.

South Street, *c.* 1900. This *is* South Street even if the postcard's caption calls it The Square. The tall building at the far end of the street is the old Crewkerne Hospital, also seen above.

St Bartholomew's church, 3 August 1894, when the bells had been taken down for re-hanging and re-framing.

Court Barton, *c.* 1902, was formerly known as Gould's Barton. Shelle House, the main building to the left, was built in 1893, the house next door was a shop at one time; note the lighter, bricked-in area which was the shop window. Early in the twentieth century, with the advent of the motor car in Crewkerne, it became a garage, and still is to this day. It is interesting that the two separate colours of slates on the roof are still there. Jubilee Cottage, with its large name-stone above the door, was built at the time of Queen Victoria's Golden Jubilee in 1887. There appears to be a house next door again but, if so, it is no longer there.

Chubbs Lawn originally belonged to the Carnival Committee but was sold to the UDC. It was the site for sheep markets and other agricultural occasions, and today is the site of the Chubbs Lawn old people's housing estate. Here implements from Gibbs & Co (H.H. Gibbs), the local agricultural engineers, are on show around 1916. They were sole local agents for Howard's Ploughs (which could be those on the left), Bamford's well-known (celebrated) machinery, and Lister engines.

Unveiling the war memorial at Severalls, *c.* 1921. The ceremony was performed by Mr E.J. Blake, the grey-haired gentleman in front of the wreath with his back to the camera. The first of the houses on Severalls' council house estate can be seen in the background. Still with the memorial theme, this road is now called Memorial Avenue, and a tree, complete with name-plate, was planted along it for every Crewkerne man who fell in the First World War.

Market Street, 1860. Probably the first-ever picture of the Red Lion, then called a Commercial Inn, now, sadly, but hopefully not permanently, closed.

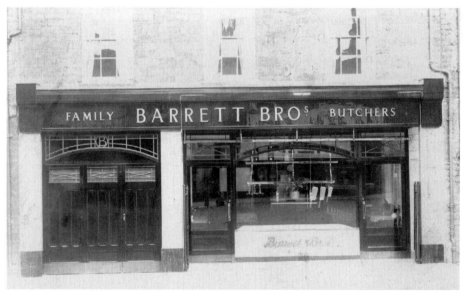

Formerly in South Street (see page 9), Barretts moved their family butchers shop to Market Street in the 1920s and, when seen here in 1928, it looks much more like the clean butchers shops today's health inspectors insist on. They had a name for their specialities such as spiced beef, home-rendered lard and home-cured bacon, and their 'noted Crewkerne Excelsior Sausages'. The premises is still a butchers shop, run for the last eleven years by Barry and John Pocock. The small lock-up on the left where there is a fish shop today was built originally as a garage.

Queen Anne's Buildings, Market Square, decorated for the coronation of King George V in 1911. The handsome building was built in 1885 and still stands today although the tower clock mysteriously vanished during the First World War. It was built on the site of the Green Dragon, one of four inns owned by Crewkerne Grammar School, and is said to have been visited by Dick Turpin. In 1911 the house on the right was owned by a local solicitor but later became Lloyds Bank. Munford was a chemists shop and for sixty years was to become Stoodley's, an undertaker and cabinet-maker. Mitchell was a draper and milliner with a good reputation throughout the area, but today his shop is the aptly named pet store, Paws, Claws and Jaws.

Demolition work around 1960 in Market Street, in progress in readiness for the new Woolworths branch.

Crewkerne Fair, 1920. Market Street was formerly called Sheepmarket Street and, although it makes it virtually impossible for modern traffic to make much progress through the street during the fair, it is a tradition that not even the police are able to prevent; the rights are buried in the fair's dim past which certainly goes back to 1279 and probably even to Saxon times. These rights were once held by the Courtenay family (who supplied the Tudor Earls of Devon who still live at Powderham), and went through several hands, including Earl Poulett's, until they were bought in 1898 by a group of prominent local people who formed themselves into a company 'for the good of the town'. It was this company that erected the Victoria Hall as it is today. The company sold Victoria Hall and Chubbs Lawn to the Urban Council and, in 1958, went into voluntary liquidation, paying out £6 for every original £5 share, although they never paid a single dividend. A new company, Crewkerne Fair and Markets Company (1958) Ltd, was formed, and registered to hold the fair rights which were not sold at the time.

Castle Inn, West Street, *c.* 1895. As the name implies, this was the road to the west, first for the London–Exeter stage-coach and the mail, including that catching the Falmouth packet, then for the trade and holiday traffic when it became the A30 trunk road. Even today, after the A303 has taken over as the London road to the west, and the advent of the M4, a considerable volume of traffic still pours along it.

West Street, *c.* 1895. The old gas lamp and the thatch on the right at the top of West Street, looking into Crewkerne, have long since gone.

The bottom of Hermitage Street, *c*. 1870.

J.H. Swaffield & Sons was founded in East Street around 1905, and is today run by a fourth generation of the family, Swaffield's great-grandsons Charles and Richard. At this date, thought to be around 1920, petrol was still being sold in cans; pumps, an American inovation, did not appear in Great Britain until the Automobile Association forced the petrol companies to adopt them by starting their own pump-operated petrol stations. Once Shell and other companies accepted the change the AA quietly bowed out.

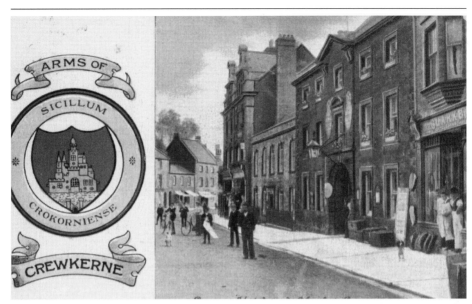

George Hotel, Market Square, *c.* 1899. We know from the message on the back of the card that the dog on the pavement is called Bobs. Neither he, nor the children in the road, would last long there in today's traffic.

Market Square looking into East Street, 1861. Hext, a pastrycook and confectioner of some repute, is now the Midland Bank. The East Street half of what was later T.R.G. Lawrence & Sons, the chartered auctioneers and estate agents, was Monkey Paull's, the hairdresser and barber. The tailor and grocers belonging to Mr G. Eyres was later Seaton & Thurgers' shop, and T.H. Bartlett's confectionery shop was to become the Army & Navy Stores. The old post office can be seen on the extreme right.

Market Street, *c.* 1900.

Market Street, *c.* 1890. Chard's shoe shop is to the left of the lamp-post. The small thatched house behind it was later demolished and, after the Second World War, became office property. The house to the right of it belonged to the Chard family and was the site of the Co-operative Society shop.

SECTION TWO

Crewkerne -
the People

Crewkerne WVS pictured outside the West Somerset Shirt Factory in Abbey Road during the Second World War. The group includes Mrs Hilda Culpitt, Mrs Fowler, Miss Burrough and Mrs Lil Ponsford.

Frank (left) and Arthur Paull at the former's wedding at St Bartholomew's church on 29 January 1949. The two brothers began playing football for Crewkerne Town in the Perry Street & District League in 1946/7 when the club restarted after the Second World War, and had contrasting twenty-year careers. Frank was a top-class goalkeeper who seldom if ever caused the referee even to check that he had his notebook with him. Arthur, who also played for Somerton, Ilminster, Chard Town, and Merriott, was a centre-forward with the hardest and deadliest shot in local football, and struck terror in opposing goalkeepers. He also had a long record of 'misunderstandings' with referees. Oddly enough Arthur, who died in June 1988, took up refereeing when he hung up his boots and quickly established himself as a no-nonsense and successful whistler – a classic example of the poacher turning gamekeeper. The highlight of both brothers' careers had to be a Perry Street League Charity Cup Final when they found themselves for once on opposing sides – Frank for Crewkerne, saving a late penalty taken by his brother Arthur, who was playing for Merriott.

Crewkerne Town Football Club in 1905/6, the season the club was formed. Back row, left to right: H. Wilson, W. Lye, S. Richards. Middle row: C. Clapp, F. England, W. Channing, H. England, F. Munford. Front row: G. Davis, W. Mundey, W. Bowditch.

Crewkerne Swifts Thursday Football Club, 1902. Many of the local workforce were engaged in the retail trade on Saturday afternoons playing their sport on a town's half-day, hence the sporting of a Wednesday or a Thursday in so many local sides' names. Back row, left to right: ? Arnold, ? Willey, ? Stringfellow, -?-, -?-, Walter Clarke, Hubert Gibbs, -?-. Middle row: ? Carter, ? Holman, F. Clarke, ? Sibley, Fred Fone, N. Raisen, A. Lacey. Front row: J. Cooper, ? Carpenter, F. Slade.

Crewkerne Horse Show, *c.* 1859. One of the oldest-known photographs of Crewkerne, this is of particular interest as it shows just how different Victoria Hall was over a century ago, and that there were actually small trees growing along the edge of the pavement on the right-hand side of the Square. Crewkerne was one of the infamous Judge Jefferey's assize towns, and it was in this square that he hanged ten local men after the ill-fated Monmouth rebellion. Victoria Hall was built as the Market House in 1730. Hodges, today's popular baker (now in the tall square building on the right) who began his business in Lyewater, was originally a cake shop and then the Empire Tea Room.

Crewkerne British Legion Carnival, 1946. The Queen, Beryle Howard, addresses the audience after her crowning. The King is Leslie Bagg, and the attendants are Betty Retland, Margarite Parsons, Peggy Samways and Cynthia Monkton.

Slade's carrier wagon at the junction of Clay Lane and Hogs Hill in Beaminster around 1890. Slade ran from Crewkerne to Bridport, connecting with many of the villages and isolated communities on the way. For the latter he was often their only contact with the outside world, carrying everything from passengers to pigs, pans and provisions. In addition to his paid work he was also the conveyor of all the local news and gossip.

Bill Slade of the Somerset Trading Company, *c.* 1931, outside Crewkerne's Swan Hotel. Bill's was a seven-day-a-week job, as even on Sunday he was expected to report for duty to feed and groom the horse. Somerset Trading had a depot at Crewkerne station from where it supplied the local farming community with all its requirements, both in feed and appliances, and stocked a wide range of building materials. In later years it was taken over by Dorset (later South-Western) Farmers Ltd.

CREWKERNE YOUNG FARMERS' CLUB.

FOURTH ANNUAL SHOW, MAY 30TH, 1939.

FIRST PRIZE

FOR

DEVON CALF

Arthur E. Stone. Hon. Secretary Advisory Committee.

This eight-cwt Devon calf reared by Miss Cynthia Newick of Higher Folly Farm, Crewkerne, was first-prize winner in its class (see above) at the 1939 Crewkerne Young Farmers' Club Annual Show held at Chubbs Lawn off West Street, now the site of the old people's houses. The animal was bought after the show by Alan Newick, the well-known Hinton St George butcher, who paid forty guineas for it – a good price but this was obviously a handsome beast. Miss Newick later married Reg Russell, the couple farming in the Crewkerne area for forty years, thirty-five of them at Folly Farm.

Crewkerne Urban District Council, 1907 – a fine body of men. Back row, left to right: C. Priddy, C.W. Haslock, M. Ewing, T. Clapp, F. Tompsett. Front: T.N. Chard, H.G. Pulleyn, W.C. Lye (vice-chairman), H. Gould (chairman), R.J. Gibbs, F. Stoodley, W.T. Isaacs.

As part of the town's celebrations during the Festival of Britain in 1951, Crewkerne Urban District Council fielded a cricket team. Standing, left to right: R. Parker (umpire), E.J. Tett (councillor), L.J. Cottrell (surveyor), E.G. Smith (surveyor's clerk) behind, K. Watson (clerk to the council), L.N. Deeley (councillor), G.H.G. Hancock (councillor), Major R.A. Russell, S. Denslow (umpire). Seated: David Tett, Dr A.M. McCall (medical officer of health), L. Taylor (council foreman), J. White (assistant clerk).

West Somerset Shirt Factory, Abbey Street, Crewkerne, *c.* 1928 (the year on the calendar is not very plain). This was the main office with, left to right, the two clerks, George Culpitt and Cyril Pinney, and the manager, Mr Cartwright. Note the pin-ups and the paint brush on the cupboard at the rear.

West Somerset Shirt Factory's cutting room. That this was a very clean, and thus much sought-after, job can be easily seen by the well-groomed workers – and only one lady among them!

Crewkerne Town Silver Band, 5 May 1923, just after its formation. Back row, left to right: George Hardy, Frank Hunt, Cyril Pike, Bill Bowden, Bert Harwood, Ern Bargery, Harry Hooper, Charles White, Vic Pinney, Charlie Genge, Will Shepherd senior. Middle row: Jack Belling, Harold Pike, Percy Rousell, Reg Pinney, Ern Pearce, Cyril Rousell, Will Shepherd junior, Fred Gosney, Eli Pinney, Edward Pinney, Jack Pearce (behind), Walter Elswood. The front row includes Sam Jones, Cliff Pavord, George Gosney, Charles Pinney, Thomas Pinney, Leslie Holderness, Will Pitts and Henry Paull.

Gibbs & Co. was founded in 1842 in Oxen Road, Crewkerne, by Robert Gibbs. The company is still in the town, albeit now in North Street on the site of the former Arnold & Hancock Brewery where the fifth generation of the family, another Robert, is managing director. His grandfather, Jack Gibbs is seen here with the firm's Morris truck at the old market field in West Street around 1926.

A mid-1920s presentation of the cup to Mr Samways of Merriott, the winner of the marathon race that was once held annually at Crewkerne on Easter Monday. Miss Sparks is presenting the cup, Police Sergeant Broom is one of three of the local force on parade.

Surely one of the biggest walking entries ever seen at any local carnival was that of the Carnival Jubilee Girls consisting of over one hundred employees of the West Somerset Shirt Factory, Crewkerne. The girls paraded in 1935 in 'costumes of red, white and blue and distinctly patriotic in honour of King George's Silver Jubilee'. They were headed in the parade by their own jazz band and their trainer Frank Sparks, undoubtedly the most envied man in Crewkerne! The girls include Ruth Tancock, Marie Lawrence, E. Pattemore, J. Pattemore, Leta and Linda Ackerman, Evelyn and Elsie Cox, M. Slade, K. Lacey, I. Lacey, L. Barter, B. Genge, O. Hooper and B. Watts.

Crewkerne Cricket Club, *c.* 1952. Left to right: Mike Slade, -?-, Tony Lawrence, Derek Apsey, Brian Apsey, Tim Udall, Nigel Swingler, -?-, Bert Apsey, Tony Davey, Alan Wright (umpire).

Swaffields' XI, Crewkerne Cricket KO Cup winners 1953. Back row, left to right: ? Iveson, Robert Gibbs, Charlie Sparkes, 'Pop' Clarke, Hedley Cornish, David Russell, Arthur Paull, George Thomas, Major Russell. Front row: Jessie Denslow, Bill Swaffield, Bert Apsey, Reg Foulds.

Crewkerne Volunteer Band (2nd Battalion Somerset Light Infantry) at Aldershot, where they took part in massed-band performances on the occasion of Queen Victoria's first Jubilee. The six band members, W. Leach, Edward Sibley, John England, B. Spearing, W. Turner and Thomas Sibley (the conductor), held a reunion fifty years later at Thomas Sibley's home at Westover in Crewkerne, when they were photographed in exactly the same positions as they were here.

The Crewkerne Volunteers, 2nd Volunteer Battalion PASLI (Prince Albert's Somerset Light Infantry, better known as 'Prince Albert's Own'), probably at camp on Salisbury Plain around 1903. The military buff will not only have noted that the sergeants are wearing their red sashes the 'wrong way' around, but will also know that this was a singular honour allowed the senior NCOs of the regiment as a tribute to a battle in India when all the officers were killed and the sergeants took charge.

B Company 2nd Volunteer Battalion PASLI at West Down, Salisbury Plain, 1900. The men, who all came from Crewkerne, Chard and the neighbouring villages, were in readiness for a call to service in the Boer War. Back row, left to right: W. Paull, W. Frost, P. Stoodley, W. Cooper, T. Rendell, J. Pearce, E. Tett, F. Hill, J. Harwood, F. Rendell, F. England, A. Shepherd, J. Prince, F. Bargery, T. Taylor, T. Parsons, F. Croft, A. Hutchings, ? Barrett. Middle row: D. Jones, G. Fowler, F. Paull, R. Roulf, A. Parsons, W. Collins, C. Butters, N. Chard, Colonel Gifford, Lieutenant A.R. Hayward, Sergeant T. Matthew, T. Stoodley, F. Wey, W. Brown, W. Hill, J. Barnes, H. Dyer, J. Sweet. Front row: Tom Lye, C. Pattemore, W. Bowden, Benny Goocoo (?), T. Pattemore, W. Chant, E.A. Sibley, H. Larcombe, W. Fowler, Sid Genge, ? Fairall. Perhaps the cycles are part of the early mechanization of the regiment.

STUDIOS
NOW OPEN
Weddings —
— Portraits —
— Commercial
145 SOUTH STREET
(rear of "County Mail" Office)
CREWKERNE :: 'PHONE 37

County Mail

and **SIMPSON CLOTHES**
Fone & Stagg's
Market St. CREWKERNE
and 43 Middle St. YEOVIL
Crewkerne 468   Yeovil 792

Head Office:
South Street, Crewkerne
'Phone 37

and Business Magnet
Established 1875

London Office:
120 Lewisham Way, S.E.14
'Phone: TIDeway 1896

No. 2587. Registered at G.P.O. CREWKERNE. Thursday, 6th March, 1958. Price 2d.

:: Chard Topics ::

ILMINSTER METHODIST CONCERT

: Crewkerne Topics :

" Ellie in Fairyland " was the title of this pretty play given by Junior girls of the Ilminster Methodist Sunday School at the Coronation concert held last Saturday.

Chard Topics

IF A suggestion that the Perry Street Carnival be held in October is adopted, it will no longer be known as the Guy Fawkes Carnival—having always previously been held in November. Last year's carnival was a huge success—and it is hoped that it will be even more successful this year.

MEMBERS of the Hawks Troop of Chard School Scouts discovered a cave last year in North East Devon, which they called Hawks' Hole. Recently they have discovered another cave in the same area which has caused much excitement and they have named it Raiders' Rift—after the patrol of advanced Scouts in the Chard School Troop. It has been only roughly explored and is said to be 700 feet in length, and it is thought that all the obvious passages have been penetrated. Many places, of course, may lead to further extensions after the removal of boulder and mud! There are eight chambers of some eighty feet in height, one of which has been named the Bats' Chamber owing to twelve bats being found there. The Raiders who took part in the discovery were R. Winch, P. Temple-West, S. G. D. Foxall and P. Tarbes—all seniors of the troop.

SOMERSET County Council have approved a 14/4d. rate which has been recommended by the finance committee. The chairman of the Committee and of the County Council, Mr. Arnold Whittaker, has described the county's financial position as one of moderate strength. Speaking of income prospects, he said: "Against expectations...

(Continued on back page)

Crewkerne Topics

MERRIOTT Bowling Club is undergoing some difficulties at the moment—owing, partly, to general lack of interest in the village. The committee are, naturally, concerned, to say the least, and since the caretaker has left no one has come forward to take his place. Surely the bowling interest has not completely died in Merriott and it is hoped that this week's annual general meeting will do something to stir up more interest in this pleasant, summer pastime.

MANY of the older residents will remember Miss Dora Sissons, S.R.N., of Seaborough, who died recently at the home of her sister, Mrs. Penn, 34 Harlington Road, Feltham, Middlesex, after much suffering. The family lived at Seaborough up to nine years ago —until the death of Miss Sissons' parents. In her early days, Miss Sissons joined the Baptist Missionary Society and was stationed at Dr. Farrars' Hospital, in India, returning about 1929 owing to ill-health, but she continued Deputation and other Christian service as her strength allowed.

WITH Easter only a few weeks ahead, the days getting noticeably longer and the first signs of Spring appearing in the gardens, the vast array of fair-weather

(Continued on back page)

CONFIRMATION AT CREWKERNE

The Lord Bishop Suffragan of Taunton, the Right Rev. Mark Hodson, will administer the sacrament of Confirmation at St. Bartholomew's Church, Crewkerne, on Sunday morning.

LIGHTING-UP TIMES
Thursday, 6th March 6.39
Sunday, 9th March 6.44
Thursday, 13th March 6.48

NATIONAL SAVINGS

National Savings collected in Crewkerne for week ending 1st March amounted to £3,034.

A BIG HELLO!

to all our well-wishers, including Organisers and advertisers. Although we are in complete agreement with your demands that some sort of Sheet should be published and that we agreed to start publishing next week, we are sorry to be disappointing but the best we can do is for the week after next, the

**WEDNESDAY,
MARCH 19th**

To acquaint those who don't already know it is proposed a Sheet with the forthcoming events and any adverts. These Sheets are to be issued free and delivered to every house in Crewkerne.

THOUGHT FOR THE WEEK
To improve the golden moment of opportunity and catch the good that is within our reach, is the great art of life.
—Johnson

BREAK AWAY FROM TRADITION

Somerset County Council have broken away from the tradition of holding all County Council elections on a Saturday as it is thought that in the present circumstances Thursday is the best day of the week to suit the general convenience of the electorate.

Candidates' nominations are to be in not later than noon on Thursday, 20th March and the delivery of candidates' notice for extension of hours of poll not later than noon on 22nd March. The issue of postal ballot papers should be made as soon as possible after 22nd March, and day of election and poll (if necessary) will be Thursday, 10th

The *Somerset County Mail* began in Crewkerne in 1875 as the *County Mail Advertising Sheet*, and was published by James Wheatley from his office in South Street, today the aptly named Printers Restaurant. The paper was later acquired by Frank Newton Parsons; at the time of its closure it was owned by Chas H. Rome. Being originally 'gratis', it was a forerunner of today's free newspapers but cost a penny by the time of the First World War, a price that had only risen to two pence by the time of its last edition on 6 March 1958, a copy of which is shown here. Afterwards it again briefly tried to run as a free paper.

Crewkerne Fire Brigade, *c.* 1926, in Church Street opposite the fire station. Jack Gibbs is on the running board; others include Jim Moerton, the leading fireman, Fred Hopper and Harry Bridge.

Crewkerne Fire Service distinguished itself during the Second World War, seeing much service during the raids on Plymouth, Exeter, Bristol and Southampton. Among the members seen here in November 1942 are Tom Bridge, Syd Tucker, Fred Knight, Fred Hooper, Ron Froom, the Roberts sisters (women were well represented and gave outstanding service), Mr Wilkins, Mr Hooper, Roland Sibley, Ron Symes and Jack Gibbs (leading fireman).

Crewkerne scouts at camp at Ladram Bay near Sidmouth, 16 August 1950. Back, left to right: George Hassel, Terry Dodge. Front: Cecil Thompson, Gerald Rodford, Roy Vaux (now a pilot with Trans-Australian Airways), and Pat Nye (now a professor at the College of California).

Members of the 1st Crewkerne Boy Scout Troop, known as Lord Poulett's Troop, pose on 4 July 1911 before leaving for London to attend the review by King George V in Windsor Great Park. Included in the group are scouts Fowler, Fone, Walden, Pike, Wey, Ewing, Bargery, Trenchard, Masters and Hansford.

Arthur Hart & Son, Station Road, *c.* 1920. Including a view here from the works' gates, the firm at the time was the largest webbing manufacturers in the West Country, making much of the webbing for the upholstery trade as well as reins and girths for racehorses, bindings and fringes for cocoa matting and carpets, seamless woven bags, and mats and belts for military uniforms.

Crewkerne Salvation Army Band, *c*. 1895 – not the smiling faces one has come to expect from the always-cheerful Sally Ann.

Crewkerne Town Silver Band, 1928.

South Street's children's coronation party on the old cricket ground, June 1953. Among the many happy faces may be seen the Davies brothers (Royston, Kenny and Alan), Alan Hunt, Valerie Harwood, Cheryl and Mary Sparks and their brother John, Hazel and Ruth Brunt, Christine Bowditch, and Jean and Wendy Russell. The party was held in the skittle alley at the Railway Tavern in South Street where (below) a feast awaited the children after the outdoor part of the proceedings, including the sports, had been completed. In the background can be seen the chimney and buildings of the old Crewkerne Gas Works.

The Railway Tavern entry for the Crewkerne Carnival around 1954 lines up for the judging in South Street. On the float, left to right: Arthur Mullins, Dave Pettitt, George Nicholls, Bill Masters, Brian Meecham, Bill Sparks, Roy Caddy, Gerald Russell, Eric Bowditch. Standing in front are Dick Caddy, the driver, and Bill Hawker.

Ralph Reader, of *Gang Show* fame, is one of Crewkerne's most famous sons, having been born at Gould's Barton off Church Street. He frequently returned home and is seen here, fourth from right standing at the top table, at a dinner in the now-closed Red Lion around 1954. Also in the picture are two of his aunts, Mrs Wally Denslow and Mrs Fred Trott, both with their husbands; Horace Pinney, sitting back in left-hand side row, then the chairman of Crewkerne UDC; Ken Watson the town clerk; and Eric Hopwood, local staff reporter for *Pulmans Weekly News* for over thirty years.

The war memorial at Severalls (see page 19) names the men of the town that did not come back from the First World War; this picture shows the ones that did. All Crewkerne's men who served as soldiers or sailors, some still in uniform, were on parade outside Victoria Hall in 1919. There is a note on the back of the original picture which states 'standing centre, Reggie Symons, Westminster Bank Manager, not a soldier'. Presumably, therefore, he was a welcoming dignitary, possibly from the council.

Crewkerne RAOB, *c.* 1954. The local lodge, the Pride of Crewkerne Lodge of 'the Buffs' as they are universally and affectionately known, here at the Swan Inn, include Ernie Shoemark, Bill Saint, Ivor Roberts, Wilf Holt, Ron Tuck, Jack Coles, Bert Cox, Freddy Hawker, Bill Murray and Wally Jeffery. The lodge was formed on 27 May 1922, meeting first at the Kings Arms, but subsequent headquarters have been at the Swan, White Horse, Red Lion and currently the Nags Head.

George Meecham, landlord at the Sawyers Arms in Crewkerne, started a general stores in South Street in June 1928 which is still run by his son Brian and daughter-in-law Doreen. George is seen here beside his Commer delivery van which, besides the pots, pans and brushes on the roof and the carpets tied to the bonnet and mudguards, contained a large paraffin tank from which he made regular deliveries around the Crewkerne area. He purchased the van around the beginning of 1939 and soon afterwards, in the early months of the Second World War, it was commissioned by the authorities and used as an ambulance, seeing service during the Plymouth blitz. It never returned to Crewkerne.

The bell-ringing team at St Bartholomew's parish church, *c*. 1948. Left to right: Myra Tancock, Tony Harper, Doreen Tancock, Revd Thomas, Harold Pike, Ray Eason, Michael Hogan, Beryl Dudley, Bert Ash, Marjorie Pike, Godfrey Pike.

Men's Branch, Crewkerne Toc H, pose to say goodbye to their padre, Revd Thomas, outside St Bartholomew School prior to his departure for Australia in 1949. Crewkerne Toc H received its lamp as a full branch on 6 June 1931 when it was lit at Crystal Palace by the Prince of Wales (later Edward VIII) and received by Garnett Cook. The branch was a male-only domain until the introduction of a now-flourishing women's section soon after the Second World War. Back row, left to right: Harry Davis, Reg Watts, Ted Hann, Pattemore, -?-, Bertie Ashworth, Garnett Cook, Mr Hancock, Police Sergeant Smith, Hugh Studley, Eric Parker, Mr Strawbridge, Mr Gussell, Mr England. Front row: Cyril Male, ? Creed, Tommy Hallett, Revd Thomas, Mr Scott, Mr Lloyd, Mr Usher, Major Russell.

Crewkerne Brewery outing, *c.* 1900. The first of at least two carriages leaves the brewery at Ashlands, off North Street, which was partially demolished in February 1960. The transition from horse-drawn to horse-powered conveyances can easily be seen; put an engine in front of this carriage and lower the wheels, and you have the charabanc of the almost immediate future.

The dedication of Crewkerne's new Morris Commercial ambulance in 1944 in the Square outside Victoria Hall. Despite the rain a sizeable crowd, including the choir, has gathered to watch the event.

Charles Russell with his son Reg (on leading horse) harvesting wheat in 1932 at Manor Farm, Wayford, near Crewkerne, where he farmed for over twenty years.

1st Crewkerne Boys Brigade, who were re-formed in 1968 at the North Street Baptist Church by Revd Sister Connie Lockwood, Captain N. Pinney, and Lieutenants M. and P. Chard, are seen shortly afterwards on parade at the junction of Church Street and Market Street. It is of interest to note the change in businesses in even such a relatively short time: SWEB has become Barclay's Bank; the empty premises next-door, in the process of becoming International Stores, is now Bath Travel; and Boots is Loders, a butchers shop.

Clapton and Crewkerne WI group was formed in 1949 and met at the old 'Clapton Hut' as the old village hall was known before being replaced by the present hall in the early 1960s. Among those at a group birthday party held in the hut around 1952, to which members from the neighbouring Misterton and the Drimpton groups were invited, are the president, Mrs Vera Williams (seated fifth from left) and the secretary, Mrs Trixie Thomas, on her left. Others include Cynthia Russell, Mrs Mabel Stoodley, Mrs 'Grandma' Stoodley, and Annie Russell, founder-member and still an active participant today in her ninety-sixth year.

The first-ever Crewkerne Hospital Cup Final, 28 April 1910. Crewkerne Town, by now nicknamed 'The Tigers' because of the yellow and black striped shirts they had adopted a few seasons earlier, had beaten Crewkerne Unitarians 2-0, Beaminster 7-0 and then lost 1-0 in the semi-final to Boden & Co., the Chard works' team. Bodens met Petters United, the forerunners of today's Yeovil Town in the final and, after 1-1 and 2-2 draws, were beaten 2-1. The three finals were all played on the Crewkerne Town ground and netted gates of £16, £11 and £18. Here the Petters team pose with the cup after the third game. Note the linesman's flag. The gentleman behind the cup is thought to be Mr George Dyson of Merriott who donated the cup; on his left is a hospital manager.

Crewkerne Grammar School, *c.* 1917.

Severalls Bowling Club, Crewkerne, *c.* 1948.

The Railway Tavern skittle team celebrate a championship around 1958 in the alley at the popular South Street public house. Standing, left to right: Herbert Spearing, 'Spuddle' Taylor, Bert Tuck, Bill Masters, George Nicholls, Arthur Mullins (landlord 1939–62), Frank Paull, Wilf Holt, 'Flo' Lawrence, Arthur Paull, -?-. Sitting: Tubby Coombes, Alan Newick, Bill Hawker, Bill Sparks, Harry Adams, Ken Bartlett (landlord of the White Lion), Bert Westcott.

SECTION THREE

Shepton and Petherton

The Square, South Petherton, *c.* 1900. On the right was the post office run by Mr Hocken; in the centre, in what is now the Blake Hall, Mr Anstice's shop has pots and pans on display in the window above.

The Davies family ran a shop in the Market House from the 1890s until just before the Second World War, trading as 'an iron monger, cutler, plumber, painter, glazier and paper hanger'. Pictured here around 1910 are, left to right: Sophia Davies (the wife of the proprietor Frederick James), her son Hugh, daughter Lilian and other son Frederick William. The lady between the two children in the porch is the family housekeeper.

The Davies family (see above) shortly before the First World War. Back, left to right: Lilian May, Frederick William and Hugh Harwood. Front: Frederick James and his wife Sophia Ann.

St James Street, South Petherton, *c.* 1903.

Judging by the other decorations this is the Christmas display outside John Gifford Corry's butchers shop in Market Square, South Petherton around 1905, shortly after his move there in 1902 from Watergore. By 1923 he had moved again, this time to West Street.

The NatWest Bank, St James Street, South Petherton in 1920 when it was known as the London County, Westminster and Parr's Bank.

South Petherton, *c.* 1943. During the Second World War this building (now the post office) was where local women made wireless valves that went to a factory in Ilminster.

South Petherton, *c.* 1890. Henry Baker, who ran a general store at the bottom of Roundwell Street, is pictured outside his shop.

Herbert Batstone, who later moved to The Knapp at Merriott (see page 157), had a bakery beside the brook in Butt Lane (or Silver Street) known as the Palace Bakery from 1904 to 1906, and was one of four bakers in the village at the time. He is seen here with his wife Alice and daughters Ada and Winnie (in her father's arms), probably in 1905. The bakehouse is at the rear but seems to share a chimney with the house and shop which fronts on to the road. Bread can be seen in the delivery cart on the left driven by an unknown 'lad'.

South Petherton, May 1937. The White sisters, Eve and Margaret, seen outside with their decorations for George VI's coronation, ran their chemists shop in St James Street for many years. When they retired in 1971 the shop was closed and everything left as it was. When it was eventually sold in 1987 the contents were auctioned and all the fittings, together with over three hundred drug jars, cartons for herbal remedies (animal as well as human!), tins, catalogues, price lists, prescription books and invoices, were sold. The majority were bought by Flambards Theme Park in Cornwall where they have been arranged just as they used to be in the shop.

The window of Dike's Bakery in St James Street around 1920. Today it is the Old Bakehouse Restaurant.

South Street, South Petherton, *c.* 1912. This postcard, postmarked 16 August 1920, displays the late use of South Petherton's 'squared-circle' postmark, a type that went out of general use around 1908 at the latest in most British towns.

South Street, South Petherton, around 1901, showing Edwin Clarke's highly reputed linen draper's establishment.

South Street, South Petherton, *c.* 1910. On the left, Pollie Hines's thatched grocery shop closed down after the First World War and was demolished in the 1960s. Mrs Hines was also an agent for a gloving factory and insisted that you spent the money in her shop which was not particularly popular because, like the 'company stores' of the song, her prices were said to be rather high.

The Square, South Petherton, *c.* 1957. Hutchings & Cornelius Bus Office (H&C) is on the left, the Crown Hotel in the centre.

Silver Street, South Petherton, *c.* 1902. The high pavements, a feature of South Petherton, were said to be a precaution against flooding.

St James Street, South Petherton, *c.* 1950.

Judging by the car number plates this picture was taken in the mid-1950s. It shows the schoolchildren walking along St James Street to the Blake Hall for their dinner. In 1991 the Somerset Education Committee stopped their school meals service, so now the children eat their sandwiches at the school.

Little Petherton, West Street, South Petherton, seen here around 1910. It was almost a separate community, with tiny houses and not-so-well-off people, and only one tap serving all the houses for which they had to cross the road. In those days there was an annual refuse collection and, as poor families threw very little away but did not want to advertise just how poor they were, the Vile children went out late at night and took rubbish from other people to put with their own. In the picture Mrs Anne Vile and Mrs Sarah Marsh are standing outside their houses.

Mrs Mary Parker, who had twelve children, is seen here around 1910 with three of her sons, Roger, Jim and John, Jim's wife, Alice, and some of her grandchildren: Fred and Will Long, Freddy Dunstone and one of Will Parker's daughters.

Petherton men having a leg-stretch stop during one of the early charabanc outings from the village around 1920. Left to right: -?-, Reg Keetch, Taylor, Will Keetch, Tom Baker, Fred Scott, Reg Best and Louis Louch.

Worsley Walters and his belt-driven Triumph motorcycle, *c.* 1903.

Baker & Sons, road contractors, at work in South Street, South Petherton in 1904. Most of their road-improvement machinery would have been made locally by the Phoenix Engineering Company of Chard who already enjoyed a nationwide reputation in this field.

East Lambrook, 1905. Mr Cheeseman and Fred Perry at work with the Patent Applepicker, known locally as the 'Hedgehog'. This weird and wonderful contraption was used for picking apples off the ground after they had been shaken from the trees; it was certainly far too cumbersome to lift up. Any bruising of the fruit would hardly matter as most of the apples were going for cider-making either by the farmer concerned or to cider-makers such as Whiteways at Whimple.

This is one of the very first cars seen in South Petherton, and must date from about 1903. The daring passengers paid sixpence for a ride along Bridge Street and back along the Coach Road (later the A303). Charlie Sweet is standing in front of the car.

South Petherton Band, 1906, including P. Gentle, Joseph Wines, William Gaylard (bandmaster), Tommy Callow, Tom Baker and Bert Hillard.

South Petherton Fire Brigade, *c.* 1905. This must have been a thrilling sight going flat out along the local lanes with two horses for speed. Around the First World War the brigade moved into the motor age converting their appliance so that it could be towed behind Will Scott's coal lorry, a move that was said to work admirably as long as he was not down at Martock station collecting coal. Left to right: John Corry (holding the horses), Worsley Walters, Joe Baker, -?-, Fred Scott.

Petherton's fire brigade at work in 1924 when the thatch and upper floor of the Bell Inn (later Brewers Arms) were destroyed by fire. Hopefully Will Scott was not down at Martock at the time, otherwise he might have had a job getting through the crowd. The pub was rebuilt the following year.

South Petherton Football Club, Ilminster Charity Cup winners 1924/5. Back row, left to right: Charlie Harwood, Jack Walker, Alf Stallard, Phil Brown, Bert Talbot, Albert Harwood, Ernie Masters, Bill Wembridge. Front row: Frank Hillard, Seymour Tucker, Ernie Giles (captain) Fred Bailey, Walt Masters.

The Blake Hall, the Square, South Petherton under construction in 1911. Some fourteenth-century cottages were demolished to make way for it, a move that was not greeted with universal approval. Among the objectors were the Taunton-based Somerset Archaeological Society who said 'Blake of South Petherton has bought the houses for £300 and proposes to build a Liberal Club on the site'. Few would argue with the fact that the plain-looking hall was a poor exchange for some lovely old cottages.

Bridge House, South Petherton, seen here around 1912, was built by William Blake in 1859 and lived in by his family until 1932 when William Harvey Blake died leaving a widow and three children, Seymour, John and Anna. The house was too big and expensive for Mrs Blake to maintain so she moved with her family to London. During the Second World War the house was let to Crohamhurst School, Croydon and then sold to Somerset County Council. No longer needed by the council and too big for anyone to want to buy it, it was dismantled in 1959, and the stone and fittings sold. Seymour Blake aquired some items and took them next door to Old Bridge, which had been in the family since 1855. The façade of Bridge House was bought for a house at Canford Cliffs, Bournemouth. Today the grounds are occupied by a mobile home park.

Workmen pause for a picture during the installation of the new water main through Watergore, c. 1908. Picture the crew today in the middle of the same road – the busy A303 London–West Country trunk road.

The Girls' School staff, November 1915. Left to right: Miss May Davies, -?-, Miss Lucy Drewer, Miss Emily Payne (headmistress), Irene Rider (pupil teacher), -?-, Evelyn White (pupil teacher).

The annual Christmas party at the convent, Compton Durville, *c.* 1960. Back, left to right: Minnie Wakely, Margery Garrett, Arthur Allen, Connie Rice, Kathleen Wakely, Margaret Allen, Arthur Fry, Barbara Fry, Carol Wakely, Roger Marsh, Mary Brain. Middle: -?-, Ardis Wakely, -?-, Keiron Marsh, -?-, Philip Marsh, Rodney Brain. Front: Teresa Rice, Arlene Wakely, Sarah Wakely, Erica Rice, Mandy Fry, David Fry, Nicholas Wakely, Louise Wakely, Martin Brain.

South Petherton Boys' School footballers, 1935. Back row, left to right: Mr Griffiths, Ken Wembridge, Les Pantling, Alan Irish, Doug Palmer, Ken Masters, Fred Taylor, Ern Saint, Bill Temlet, Mr Smyth. Middle row: Sid Williams, Roy Brown, Bern Priddle, Bryn Best, Ken Hooper, Jack Pantling, Tony Best. Front row: Ken Harris, Ted Benjafield, Dick Keetch, Den Gummer, Roland Gundry, Harold Cridland.

In 1911 the Wheatsheaf Inn, on the Corn Hill in the Square at South Petherton, needed rebuilding. Rather than close down and lose the licence, the landlady, Mrs Gilesy, decided to move her family down to Hele Lane but keep the pub open while the work was being done. The picture shows the new roof which had been erected over the old building while it was being demolished and then rebuilt.

A service at the war memorial, South Petherton. Lord Harding is in uniform on the left; Walter Harris holds the wreath.

St James's church bells, South Petherton, receiving attention from T. Blackbourne, the Salisbury bellhangers. This fine minster church was restored both in 1861 and 1879.

Joseph Cornelius, seen here in 1894 when aged sixty-one, was a popular Shepton Beauchamp performer. It was at this time that he sang three songs to Cecil Sharpe, the well-known collector of English folk dances and songs, who published two of them the following year. Note the baby board at the foot of the door, a common sight at the time.

Shepton Beauchamp School, 1912–13. Judging by the well-turned-out appearance of the children and the 'Never Absent' caption on the photo, they have paraded to receive prizes for 100 per cent attendance during the school year. Only the little girl, centre above the front row of stern young men, seems to be pleased with herself.

Shepton Beauchamp Union of Agricultural Workers, skittle shield winners, 1946/7. Back row, left to right: William Cornelius, Ed Rowswell, Jack Clark, Tom Cornelius, Tom Welch, Bert Cornelius, George Pond. Front: Kenneth Welch, Harry ' Josher' Cornelius, Walter Marks.

The Hospital, South Petherton, *c.* 1939. It was built as an isolation hospital in the mid-1930s but no one seems to know who was being isolated, or why. Still very much in use today, it is now used mainly for patients who are convalescing.

The Shambles, Shepton Beauchamp, *c*. 1910. Rowswell's butchers shop is still there but the door has been altered into an archway to allow vehicle access.

The Shambles, Shepton Beauchamp, probably taken around the same time as the picture above, but looking in the opposite direction, as the gentleman with the rake is in both. He was employed to sweep a crossing and to keep the village streets generally clean and tidy. The high pavements that are so common in Shepton Beauchamp are said to be a safeguard against flooding.

Alfred Cornelius started work as a stonemason working on the breakwaters at Brixham and Portland, actually cycling to the latter job. In 1930 he began operating a coach business from the Royal Oak at Barrington, later joining forces with Tommy Hutchings of South Petherton to form the well-known Hutchings & Cornelius coach firm whose trading title H&C was fondly, if rudely, interpreted by all and sundry as either 'Hot & Cold' or 'Horse & Cart'. The main reason for the merger of the two five-coach fleets was the added purchasing power it gave them. The firm operated until 1978. Alfred Cornelius is seen here at the South Petherton office around 1950.

A Hutchings & Cornelius coach outside the Royal Oak, Barrington, *c.* 1937. It was garaged in the shed to the right which is now a lawnmower repair business. The occasion for the picture was that Charles Cornelius, having come of age at twenty-one, and thus old enough to take the test for bus drivers, is about to have his first 'solo' drive. Left to right: Fred Bridge (Alfred Cornelius's first driver), Alfred Cornelius, his son Charles and wife Emily. Charles, who became a conductor at the age of thirteen, drove coaches for forty-nine years before eyesight problems caused him to retire aged seventy.

Charlie Jeffery, pictured in 1940 with the Hutchings & Cornelius coach on which he worked as a conductor. Later he left to join Standard Telephones Company at Dowlish Ford near Ilminster.

One of Hutchings & Cornelius's 30hp coaches at Barrington in 1936.

Shepton Beauchamp Football Club, 1961/2. Members of the Perry Street & District Football League at the time, the club was about to embark on its most successful post-war era, winning their first-ever championship that season, the first of three such successes in five years. The team pictured here is the one that beat Crewkerne 2-0 in the Coronation Cup Final on Boxing Day 1961 with late goals from Derek Pitman and Mike Pearce. Back row, left to right: Ivan Margetts, Bernard Welch, Gerald Wakely, Dave Gard, Barry Perry, David Jackson. Front row: Derek Pitman, Gordon Male, David Wakely, Mike Pearce, Terry Cornelius.

Shepton Beauchamp School, 1928. Back row, left to right: Ken Dinham, Bernard Wakely, Basil Meade, Fred Cornelius, Hugh Gummer, Arthur Symes, Bill Salisbury. Middle row: Phyliss Meade, Glen Bealey, Daisy Drayton, Gwyneth Rowswell, Kathleen Budge, Gwen Brown, Lily Cornelius, Edith Light. Front row: Billy Hawkins, Eddie Rowswell, Frank Watts, Donald Allen, Wilfred Budge.

Shepton Beauchamp Football Club, c. 1923, pictured in the Crat Field. At the time Shepton was competing in the Yeovil & District League and, being what might politely be called 'a man's team', had a robust outlook to the game, being nicknamed 'The Monsters'; they proudly displayed the fact on the ball in this picture. Back row, left to right: Owen England, Tom Rowswell, Bert Drayton, Cyril Hawkins, Len Harris, Harry Bridge, Will Harris, Ned Welch, Bert Rowswell, John England, Norman Grey. Front row: Fred Newman (trainer), Arthur Harris, Tom England, Herb Harris, Stanley Rowswell, Ed England, Anthony Rowswell (linesman).

Shepton Beauchamp Girl Cuides, c. 1964. The captain is Miss Tatham, the lieutenant Miss Woodard. The troop included girls from Barrington, Lambrook and other local hamlets.

The Shambles, Shepton Beauchamp, *c.* 1938. This card was sent home to Wales during the war by an airman serving at the then Royal Air Force station at Merrifield, now HMS Hermes, a helicopter field. The Duke of York pub is on the right. The Shambles are sixteenth century and the turning to the right (Great Lane) is the Barrington road.

Silver Street, South Petherton, *c.* 1905, taken on the high pavement looking towards Martock. On the left is Christmas Cottage and the old Rope Walk; today the entrance to the Stoodham housing estate is between them. On the right the first cottage has gone, beyond it there is a shop which was owned by the Harding family for many years and was used as a grain store for the bakery during the Second World War.

Norman Henry Hawkins with his baker's delivery cart at Shepton Beauchamp around 1947. Hawkins, who covered the Shepton and Barrington districts daily, was a popular man locally, not least for the excellent service he provided in cooking Sunday and Christmas dinners in his ovens.

Local butcher Henry Bond, who once had a slaughterhouse at The Old Thatch in Love Lane, Shepton Beauchamp, is pictured here on his round at Kingsbury Episcopi around 1938.

Revd Arthur Lethbridge, a much-loved rector of Shepton Beauchamp for forty-seven years (1885–1932), who died in office.

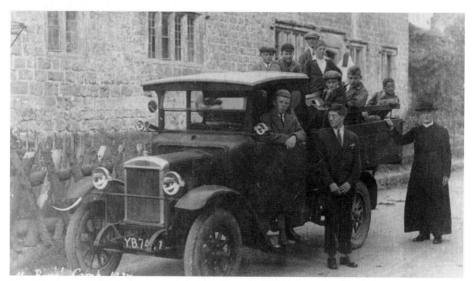

Revd Arthur Lethbridge with the Shepton Beauchamp Boys Brigade outside Tudor House in 1927 prior to their departure on an outing. Note the wooden seats in the back of Mr Hobart Cornelius's Morris truck; it was also a coal lorry and the seats were removable (and hopefully washable!).

Cornelius Cornelius and his wife Annie pictured at Shepton Beauchamp in 1914 with six of their seven children. The girls, left to right, are Rose, Sarah and Violet, the boys William, Harry and Reg. Edith is the missing daughter.

Shepton Beauchamp, *c.* 1960. The Seavington Hunt moves off past the post office and Hawkins' shop in North Street where, despite the parked cars including a 1960 Cortina, traffic was still not a problem.

Barrington Football Club, 1952/3. That season Barrington, who won the Perry Street &
District League's Intermediate Section (North), the equal of today's Division One, stunned
league circles with the greatest giant-killing acts in league history. Not once, but four
times in the League Charity Cup (since renamed the Challenge Cup), they were drawn
against teams from the division above them. And four times they won, including two wins
over local 'Ham Stone Country' rivals: by 3-2 in the semi-final against Stoke under Ham,
who that season were to win what would prove to be the second of four successive
championships, and then by 3-1 in the final at Martock against Crewkerne Town who
finished runners-up to Stoke. Barrington, who scored through Bernard Hopkins, Clifford
Male and Ron England, played the last thirty-nine minutes without Hopkins who had
suffered a broken nose; in those days there were no substitutes. The team and officials are
pictured with the Perry Street League Charity Cup, the Somerset Intermediate Cup and the
League Championship Cup. Back row, left to right: Charlie Bond, Eric Woodland, Roy
Clarke, Ron Cornelius, Alan Martin, Ron England, Fred Bond, Les Nunn, Hughie Dade.
Front row: Les Bond, Raymond Cook, Terry White, 'Ginger' Board, Clifford Male, Geoff
Pearce, Bernard Hopkins.

Henry Bond takes time off from hoeing a root crop in Higher Field, Webber's Farm, Barrington around 1927, to pose with three young ladies who found a roller a convenient platform to show their charms. Left to right they are Dorothy Cornelius, Gladys Cornelius and Doris 'Doll' Bond.

Barrington Football Club on a ground probably at Barrington Court in the early 1920s when they competed in the Yeovil & District League. Back, left to right: Bert Dade, Len Cook, Kelly Male, -?-, Fred Meade, Alf Cornelius, -?-. Front: Fred Brickhard, -?-, Fred Bond, Fred Male who was to give many years service as a local referee when he gave up playing, Stanley Cornelius (back), Fred Pittard, -?-, -?-.

Barrington Carnival, *c.* 1948. Fred Morris, as the lady, and Wilf Bond on their way to the judging. They are posing where today's Sharland council house estate was built.

Great Park Field, Barrington Court, *c.* 1930. Known to have been used exclusively for pasture during the past half-century, this huge field at Barrington Court appears to have been used for cereal growing in earlier years. Effram Bartlett, Henry Bond (centre and well-known for his wart-charming properties), and an unknown third man on the right are at work, with not a cider jar in sight. Despite the world lead in mechanization which British agriculture enjoyed by this time, it was still a common sight in the 1930s to see mowing teams at work, especially in the West Country.

SECTION FOUR

Martock, Stoke and Norton

Bower Hinton, Martock, *c.* 1901.

H.W. Hebditch & Co. Ltd, Martock, was certainly the West Country's and probably the country's leading manufacturer of wooden buildings, specializing in poultry and general farm buildings. Formed in 1900 by two brothers, Harry and Charles Hebditch, the firm owed its origins to the fact that the brothers collected eggs from farms around South Petherton. To ensure a steady supply and cut out some of the middle men, they also kept their own poultry flock for which they made their own chicken-houses. These were of such a high standard that they were able to sell them and set up their business at Martock which was an instant success. They sold throughout the United Kingdom and Europe, enjoying a reputation second to none for standards and prices and, more important perhaps, were good employers of the old-fashioned, family type for three generations until Hebditch ceased trading in 1985. Pictured here around 1930, in a Hebditch-built office, of course, are Harold Hebditch, Jack Helyar, Harry Hebditch, Norman Hebditch and Mr Lewis (secretary).

The office staff at H.W. Hebditch & Co. Ltd, taken at the same time as the picture opposite. Note the typewriter and the old-fashioned coke stove, which appears to be in use at the time. Left to right: -?-, B. Mounter, -?-, Mrs Pople, H. Chant, H. Cullingford, W. Tucker, L. Triptree, Rene Dear.

Some of W.H. Hebditch & Co. Ltd's workmen outside the office with Harry Hebditch (extreme left), *c.* 1910. Obviously not in their working clothes, these men may have been going to one of the local agricultural shows at which the firm had a stand. The first three men from the right are Will Taylor, Charlie Russ and Charlie Bishop; the boy in front is probably Bill Tucker. It is interesting to note that five of the men, including the boss, are smoking.

The last train in Martock leaves the station for Taunton on 13 June 1964. The station, which, along with the entire Taunton–Yeovil line, was a victim of the Beeching Axe, was opened in 1862. This train, which is just departing for Taunton, is carrying Fred Lawrence who bought one of the last tickets ever sold at the station – a one-and-sixpenny single to Langport.

The first aeroplane in Martock, 1911. Graham Gilmour flew his Bristol Boxkite version of the Farman pusher biplane from Larkhill to Martock where he gave flying demonstrations. A year later he was killed flying from Martock to London after another display. He had offered a ride to local farmer's son Arthur Palmer whose father refused permission and probably muttered something like 'I told you so' when he heard of the fatal crash.

Polling Day, December 14th.

The favour of your Vote is solicited for

Lt.-Col. Hon. Aubrey Herbert
(Irish Guards).

He has been your Member since 1911, and has done his best to serve you both in Peace and WAR.

Printed and Published by E. Whitby & Son,
Albion Printing Works, Yeovil.

A crowd gathered at Martock to hear The Hon. Aubrey Herbert canvassing at a by-election in November 1911 at which he was successfully elected with a 144 majority as the Liberal member for South Somerset (Yeovil). Before the advent of television a candidate had to get out to every nook and cranny of a constituency and meet the people. At Martock, Herbert had been met on the outskirts of the village by a huge crowd, and escorted to the centre in a procession of motor cars, traps, and farmers on horseback. His card for the 1918 election campaign is seen above.

SOUTH SOMERSET BYE-ELECTION THE HON A HERBERT MP AT MARTOCK 30-11-11   MAJORITY 148.

Strodes Grammar School, Martock, seen here around 1910, was founded in 1661.

The Martock Carnival on 12 May 1937, as the date suggests, was held as part of the celebrations for George VI's coronation. Here the Palmer family entry prepares to leave from the Red Lion in Bower Hinton.

The staff of Yandle & Sons, Martock, pictured in 1949 include W. Paull, E. Elliott, K. Dodge, C. Best, J. English, M. Gould, E. Keel, V. Hallett, W. Lavis, S. Rogers, F. Quantock, H. Moore and Mr & Mrs Trask (centre, front row), whose silver wedding anniversary was the occasion of the picture. Yandle's was founded at Martock in 1860 by Henry John Yandle. The firm specialized in war work during the First World War.

Market House, Martock, seen here in 1923, has led a varied life since its erection in Georgian times. The building has been used as a fire station, and as a meeting place for the local council and other bodies including, as the pictures shows, the Comrades Club (a body of ex-servicemen). The Pinnacle which stands in front was erected to mark the site of a former market-place.

A Scammel steam engine driving an early baling machine at Bower Hinton Farm, Martock, in 1912. Today's health and safety inspectors would have plenty to say about the unguarded wheels and pulleys.

The Palmer brothers, Andrew and Duncan, are the fifth generation of the family to have farmed at Bower Hinton Farm near Martock over the past 150 years. Here, around 1877, their great-grandfather Walter (seated left), poses with his wife Amelia (extreme right), and their children, Arthur, Ethel and Gifford.

The funeral procession of Walter Parsons passes the Hillview council estate in Martock around 1932.

Martock Fair, 20 August 1907, at the Fairfield in Coat Road.

Bower Hinton football team, 1928/9. Back row, left to right: J. Wintle, G. Weeks, C. Sparrow, G. Marks, S. Sparrow, A. Edmunds, C. Priddle, -?-. Middle row: C. Gaylard, G. Burt, D. Steed, W. Willis, P. Baker. Front row: J. Vaughan, F. Yandle, A. Denman, P. Tulk, S. Callow.

East Street and The Cross, Martock, c. 1902.

North Street, Martock, *c.* 1954.

Norton sub Hamdon Cricket Club, *c.* 1928. Sadly the club was disbanded shortly after the Second World War after enjoying a reputation for sportsmanship for many years. Back row, left to right: Dave Brake, Will Sweet, Will Gilman, Charlie Sweet, Henry Smith, Harry Dart, -?-, Tim Hamlin, 'Doctor' Bool, Herbie Hamlin, -?-. Middle row: -?-, Bob Wills, Percy Bussel, Bert Chafey, Arch Osborne, Alec Gilman, -?-. Front row: Lewis Hamlin, Sam Hamlin, Arthur Hamlin.

The tower of St Mary the Virgin parish church at Norton sub Hamdon was struck by lightning at 4.30a.m. on 29 July 1894. The restoration work took a year and was so carefully done that although many fired stones were re-used the ninety-eight-foot tower was rebuilt to look exactly as it had done before the incident. Unfortunately the five old bells in the tower were destroyed, four of them dating from 1608 and the work of Richard Purdue of Closworth, a well-known bellfounder of the time, the fifth even older from the reign of Henry VIII. They were replaced by a ring of six bells cast by the London firm of bellfounders, John Warner & Co., in 1895. The picture shows the choir and vicar outside the church before a service held during the celebrations to commemorate the restoration. St Mary the Virgin, even in an area of outstanding churches, is a superb example of fifteenth-century work, although there are traces of an earlier Norman building. Apart from the magnificent tower, of particular interest are the church plate, the pigeon house in the churchyard and the superb roofs above the nave and the aisles.

The Wills brothers (left to right) John, Jeff and Bob, here with their father Bob (front) around 1948, were among the most talented players the highly successful Norton sub Hamdon Football Club produced. Bob senior played in Norton teams before the war, the brothers, along with a fourth brother Mike, were members of the team that was so successful in the late 1930s and especially after the Second World War. Bob (junior) gained a Perry Street League championship medal with Yeovil-based Westland Sports in 1945/6, where he had worked during the war, and returned to score 102 goals for Norton in 1947/8 including eleven in a 16-1 home win over Shepton Beauchamp Reserves. Both are club records and the 102 goals has only been beaten once in the Perry Street League's ninety-year history.

Norton sub Hamdon Football Club 1947/8, winners of the Somerset Intermediate Cup, the Chard British Legion Cup, and champions of the Perry Street & District League's intermediate section where, out of a twenty-two match programme, they won twenty-one and drew the other game. The Chard Cup success was particularly highly regarded at the time as they beat Seaton Athletic, who played in the division above them, 4-1 in the Boxing day final. Back row, left to right: S. Thorne (secretary), H. Greenham, M. Phillips, C. Best, E. Trotman, R. Holland, L. Sweet. Second row: G. Bool, G. Weakley, L. Callow, J. Wills, F. Gooding, J. McMullen, N. Aldridge, F. Raison. Front row: C. Hamlin, E. Bussell (captain), R. Wills, K. Warry, F. Trotman.

Great Street, Norton sub Hamdon, *c.* 1948.

Centenary of Norton sub Hamdon School, 1965. Mr Roy Hodges holds the cake while the children, who include Martin Hamlin, Gillian Margetts, Shani Rendall, Bob and Barry Wills, and Lorraine Hallett, try to blow its hundred candles out.

Broadmead Lane, Norton sub Hamdon, *c.* 1948.

Norton sub Hamdon, 1904. Pictures of various jubilee and coronation celebrations are far from uncommon, but this one is of a more unusual theme and finds Norton decked out with bunting and flags to mark Edward VII's seventieth birthday. Court Field is in the background.

Norton sub Hamdon Football Club dinner, 1949. Held to celebrate winning the Chard British Legion Cup, the diners include Joan Parsons, Freda Sweet, Edna Minchington, Mary Ellis, Sam Ellis, Matt Phillips, Sam Hamlin, Arthur Thorne, Bob Wills and his sons, Bob, John, Mike and Jeff. At the top table is the Perry Street League chairman F.S. 'Fred' Carpenter, third from the right.

Norton sub Hamdon School, infants' class, 1907. Sam Hamlin is second left in the front row; Tim and Charles Hamlin are first and second left in the second row and Hilda Hamlin is third left in the fourth row.

Norton sub Hamdon School, 1930. Back row, left to right: Ken Bussell, Eddy Rice, Bob Ellis, Billy Allen, Ray Snellgrove. Second row: Edna Minchington (seated), Edna Hamlin, Rose Hamlin, Betty Sweet, Ruby Bool, Joan Parsons, Elsie Johnson, Hilda Wills, Bob Wills, Miss Mayo. Third row: John Wills, John McMullen, Nelly Sweet, Tony Sweet, Fred Greenham. Fourth row: Cyril Bool, Leslie Minchington, Percy Parsons, Wilfred Osborne, Eric Osborne, Even Minchington, Gordon Bool, Miss Loxton (seated). Front row: Jim McMullen, Dennis Tanner, Joan Bool, Nelly Bool, Mary McMullen, Pat Warry, Michael Wills.

Castle Street School, Stoke under Ham, c. 1928. Charles Chant is on the extreme left in the front row.

Mr Warry was a blacksmith at Stoke under Ham for many years before the Second World War; among other prices he charged extra for 'unruly horses'.

Ellis Daniel Terrell Chant (1884–1944), the son of Daniel Chant (1826–85), pictured in the courtyard of the Duke of Cornwall Inn in Stoke under Ham around 1910; his son Evan is one of the boys with him. R. Wilmington, a well-known Edwardian photographer at East Street, Martock, took this picture.

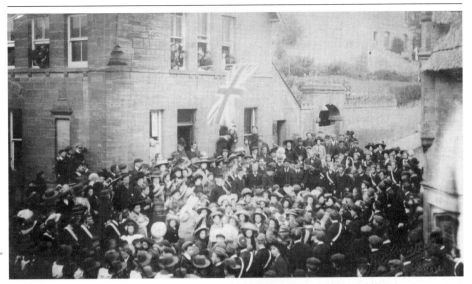

The proclamation of George V at Stoke under Ham in 1910.

The visit of King George VI on 2 January 1937 to his manor of Stoke under Ham where his tenants were presented to him. The King, who was fulfilling one of his first public engagements after his accession to the throne, is seen here leaving Summerlands between the Fleur-de-Lys and John Halter Ltd's glove factory.

John Hawkins was the first man to draw the Old Age Pension in Stoke under Ham and is seen here outside the post office holding his pension 'book' while the postmistress hands him the money. The gentleman to the right is obviously a local dignitary called in to lend substance to what, after all, was a historic moment not only in Stoke but throughout the nation. Introduced in 1909 by Lloyd George, the pension, only payable at the age of seventy, and not in full if you were already receiving £21 a year, was a great step forward in social progress.

John Hawkins (see above) worked in Stoke under Ham as an odd-job man, sweeping chimneys and emptying cess-pits. He is seen here around 1902 driving his donkey cart along High Street.

The post office, Stoke under Ham, *c.* 1906. The arched doorway to the left of the post office was the old stables but by the Edwardian era, Stoke post office had reached the motor age, albeit with the aid of bicycles for those lonely, rutted lanes along which this handsome van and its spoked and solid-tyred wheels would have ventured at considerable risk. It is interesting to note the recruiting poster beside the office door, a common sight at post offices of the time that was continued until well after the First World War (see Haslebury post office on page 137). Then the post office was at No. 3 in the High Street; today is has moved a few yards up the road to No. 9.

The Castle Street School staff in 1900 includes the headmaster Mr John Bell (seated centre row), Miss Durrant, Daniel Chant and Bertha Murley. The three girls in front, who could well be pupil teachers, are Leila Harris, Eva Chant and Mary Terrell.

The corner of North Street and High Street, Stoke under Ham, *c.* 1950, with one of the early 'split-window' Morris Minors in the days before the village was invaded by horrid yellow lines.

High Street, Stoke under Ham, *c.* 1950. Chant's Bakery is today's Tamerisk Hairdressers.

The Chapel, North Street, Stoke under Ham, probably in the 1920s. The trees behind and, of course, the gas lamp have long since gone.

Cartgate Inn was an eighteenth-century coaching inn on the old A303 road just outside Stoke under Ham; it was pulled down to make room for road improvements in 1971 when much of the A303 was being brought up to the standards required of the major trunk road from London to West Country. It took its original name, the Prince of Wales Inn, from George III's eldest son, later George IV. In the coaching era the far end of the building beside the Stoke turning was the stables. Unlike most coaching inns, however, there are no bay windows to allow would-be passengers to spot the oncoming stage.

The original Stoke Band in 1891, the year of its formation, pictured prior to leaving for Lyme Regis where it was playing on the front. Tommy Woodgate is on the extreme right at the back with the circular bass; Jessie Warry is at the other end with the drum. A journey to Lyme Regis was not such a feat as it might first seem: a short walk to the nearby Martock station, change at Yeovil and again at Axminster, and it would have been completed in no more than an hour. However, Jesse Warry with the big drum might have had something to say about the 'short' walk to Martock, and would certainly have remarked about the long climb up out of Lyme Regis back to its station.

Stoke Silver Band at Norton Flower Show, August 1955. Formed in 1891 and re-formed in 1945 after the Second World War, the band was in great demand at functions throughout West Somerset and beyond, and an all-male preserve until the arrival of Sonia Biggs, the first girl player in the mid-1960s. Back row, left to right: Bert Lawrence, David Montacute, ? Grinter, ? Andrews, Jasper Batstone, Cecil Gilman (now the band's president), David Plympton, John Williams, Elwyn Newman, Roy Blackmore, ? Cookson. Front row: Walt Shayler, Herb Montacute, Alan Richards (bandmaster for thirty years from 1950), Derek Wardle, Dick Kelloway.

Roland Waterman, managing director of the Stoke under Ham family glove-making business of John H. Walter Ltd, seated on a brand-new belt-driven Douglas motorcycle around 1906.

Times and fashions change. Stanley, son of Roland Waterman (see above) has, by the mid-1920s, graduated to a Citroën motor car.

The staff at the John H. Walter Ltd glove factory pose at Langlands. The modern-day Langland council estate begins to the right of this picture dated around 1909.

Workmen in the cutting room at John H. Walter Ltd's factory in Stoke under Ham during the 1920s. Yeovil, which is only a few miles from Stoke, was once the centre of a considerable glove trade, and at this time there were as many as fourteen glove factories in Stoke, of which Walter's was the oldest.

Ham Hill & Doulting Stone Quarry near Stoke under Ham but actually in Norton sub Hamdon, April 1922. The machine seen here was used for cutting the stone ready for planing; the shed behind once housed over a hundred stonemasons.

Quarrymen at work in the Ham Hill & Doulting Stone Company's quarries at Norton sub Hamdon in 1922. The men are preparing to cut out a block of stone from the quarry floor which, when ready, would be lifted up the 100-foot quarry face by enormous steam cranes. The quarries, used even by the Romans, have supplied much of the warm brown stone used extensively thoughout the area covered by this book and beyond; they were closed in the 1950s but reopened in 1982 by Ray Harvey and are now owned by Montagu Estates Ltd.

Stoke under Ham Congregational church anniversary parade, 14 July 1907. With only horse-drawn vehicles in sight, traffic was no problem in the High Street outside the Duke of York Hotel. Obviously the church elders were considered to be more important than Stoke Band and have taken up pole position in the parade.

Another Congregational church anniversary at Stoke under Ham, this time around 1893 but the date on the poster is faint. The local beauties have just reached the church with a floral arch which could probably have doubled as a maypole without much effort.

Although football was a serious business in Stoke under Ham in the 1920s and 1930s, especially when those arch-enemies from nearby Martock or Norton sub Hamdon were in the offing, a highlight of the year was always George Purrier's comic match at which two 'teams' battled for a cup seen here being driven in state in a brand-new 1927 Austin 7, with a Boys Brigade escort, to the old Stoke football ground for the 1927 game. The village has turned out in force for the occasion.

One of the teams for the 1927 George Purrier Cup games. Despite the intrusion of some of the fancy dress party, these players, many of whom were to make Stoke such a force in the local soccer world in the years ahead, seem to be taking it seriously.

Stoke under Ham Boys Brigade march through the village, *c.* 1906.

A chapel-gathering at Box Mount, the Stoke home of the Southcombe gloving family. Mrs Southcombe founded the chapel.

The workforce of South Harp Farm, Over Stratton, which is just off the now A303 trunk road between Stoke under Ham and Crewkerne, c. 1926. The farm, now demolished to make way for a modern housing development, was owned by the Blake family who were responsible for building the Blake Hall in South Petherton and whose connections with the Falkland Islands led to Falkland Square in Crewkerne being thus named; Les Johnson in this picture actually worked for the Blakes in the Falklands. Back row, left to right: B. Larcombe, W. Samson, F. Stone, W. Hooper, F. Radford, W. Johnson, F. Harris, H. Hooper, Mr Goskitt, L. Johnson, W. Stuckey, G. Bird. Front row: Allison Blake, Mrs Blake with her son Charles on her lap, Mr N.D. Blake (with Max his dog), Ann Trenchard (housekeeper).

Some of the workers outside the John H. Walters Ltd glove factory at Stoke under Ham around 1904.

William Rowland Waterman, managing director of John H. Walters Ltd, in his factory office around 1930.

Stoke Band leading a scout church parade down East Street in 1955.

Albert Chant (nearest camera) outside his bakers shop in High Street, Stoke under Ham, around 1930.

Albert Chant with his daughter Edna and the baker's delivery van in Stoke's High Street around 1928.

The Prince of Wales (later Edward VIII) at the entrance to Shelves on Ham Hill during a visit around 1921. A wet day has failed to dampen the walk-about and, although two long-arms of the Somerset Constabulary are on parade, security was no problem in those far-off pre-terrorist days.

The old Stoke Military Band, *c.* 1910. Back row, left to right: Jack Hartnell, Alf Dyer, Jack Baker, Harry Haines, Alwin Geard, Joe Shayler, Harry George, Bert Gillette. Middle row: Cecil Dalwood, Joe Chant, Herb Thorne, Walt Shayler, George Dalwood, Will Haines, Frank Banwell, Will Hann. Front row: Billy Dunford, Jack Rose.

Bonnings Lane, Stoke under Ham, *c.* 1930. The area to the immediate left has seen considerable development. The war memorial on the top of Ham Hill is clearly visible behind.

Stoke under Ham Cricket Club, *c.* 1900. It is interesting to compare this picture, where, if you discount the two boys on the ground, around three-quarters of the cricketers have either moustaches or a beard, with that of the footballers below, all of whom are clean-shaven.

Stoke under Ham Football Club, 1922/3. Stoke competed in the Yeovil & District League at the time, and the above team, which includes the two Chant brothers, won the Junior League, the Somerset Minor Cup and the Ilminster Charity Cup.

Stoke under Ham Cricket Club, *c.* 1920, pictured with unknown opponents at a home game. Which side scored the ultra-high, 356-run total is not known, but it is safe to assume that it was Stoke and even safer to assume that the players with smiles are not bowlers.

The Avenue, the council estate in Stoke under Ham, pictured during construction in the 1930s. Included among the workers is Bob Wills (senior).

Stoke under Ham Football Club, 1934/5. Golden ages seldom last long, and are seldom all golden, but there can be no doubt that the Stoke team that won the Perry Street & District League championship five times in a row in the 1930s, starting with the 1933/4 season, contributed some of the finest pages in the league's history. Their league record beggars description and has never been equalled before or since. In the five seasons they were almost unbeatable, and it was the ambition of every local footballer to overturn this record. In their five championship years they played 109 league games, winning ninety-two of them, drawing thirteen, and only losing four; their goal difference was 490-107, or almost 5-1 a game. Here in 1934/5, the second of their title years when they beat the Rest of the League 6-2 in the annual match with the champions, they also won the Somerset Junior Cup, and were runners-up in the Chard Hospital Cup and the Ilminster Cup. Pictured here on the old ground at Footlands are, back row, left to right, Frank Griffen, Graham Weakley, Ralph Gold, Jack Waterman (president), Bert Roles, Henry Palmer, Alf Rice (bag man); front row, Jack Holt (trainer), Horace Rockey, Fred Cooper, Ivor Whitlock, Fred Cornelius, Tommy Palmer, Wyndam 'Bob' Swain (secretary). On the ground are George Greenham and Winston Stuckey.

SECTION FIVE

Misterton and Haselbury

The post office, Haselbury Plucknett, *c.* 1925.

Haselbury Plucknett held its one and only carnival in 1972 which considering its success is surprising. This entry is 'Dave (Dave Runciman) and the "Diddy Tots"'.

The White Horse, Haselbury Plucknett, c. 1909. The bend in the road is still there but the high wall to the right of the inn has been lowered by at least half, and a small extension built inside. The cottage opposite has lost its thatch, the background trees and the rooks' nests have gone but nowadays telegraph poles have taken over.

Inside the Swan Inn, Haselbury Plucknett, *c.* 1950. The landlord Fred Churchill, with his wife Melita on his immediate right, sitting in the bar of the popular inn at the top of Swan Hill. Sydney Raison is on Mrs Churchill's right, with Tom Samways on the right of the picture.

Haselbury Plucknett Club Day, 1907. The club was a Savings Club or Friendly Society into which villagers paid a small weekly amount and were entitled to a weekly payment in times of illness. The Club Day was the highlight of the village year and the scene of much merriment, eating, drinking, dancing, games and sports. Here most of the village are posed in the field behind Oak House.

A North Perrott outing about to set off in one of Pennel King's charabancs, *c.* 1927. It is interesting to note that this vehicle, although only dated a few years after many such vehicles pictured in this book, has graduated to pneumatic tyres. Left to right: George Osborne, Clifford Parkman, Frank Sherston, Margory Parkman, Violet Ashford, Ivy Parkman, -?-, -?-, Mr Young, the driver, -?-, -?-, Alice Searle, -?-, -?-, Ern Travers. The lady and child in front are unknown.

The coronation of Elizabeth II, 3 June 1953. Among those at the children's coronation party in North Perrott Hall are Martin Elson, Phil and Mary Cook, Jean Draper, Freda Lemon, Ray Parkman, Sally Purchase and Pearl Lane. Miss Flossie Matravers on the extreme right was a much-loved Sunday school teacher in the village for over fifty years.

North Perrott, near Haselbury Plucknett, *c.* 1905. This is the classic village centre, with the village pump, the horse trough, the light and, of course, the pub. Here the Manor Arms still has its attractive sign which in later years was removed following several 'arguments' with passing lorries.

North Perrott Gardening Club outing, *c.* 1955. Pictured outside the New Buildings prior to leaving for an unknown destination, the group includes Tommy Hallett, Fred Stoodley, Mrs Stoodley, Mrs Van Willmott, Mrs Dan Willmott, Alfred Trask, Mrs Trask, Mike Docherty and Alfred Hawkins.

Reverend George Augustus Caley, vicar at St Michael and All Angels' church at Haselbury Plucknett 1883–98, in a charming family pose with his wife and two daughters.

Haselbury Plucknett pantomime, 1935. Held in the School Room to raise funds for St Michael and All Angels' parish church, a cast of twenty-five under Mr Lee staged *Aladdin* for a week and then ran it for three days in the Victoria Hall at Crewkerne. The vicar, Revd Ernest Haskins, is sitting in the front, Mrs Haskins is standing second from the right and others include Phylis Osborne, Miss Shutler, Muriel Lewer, Mollie Rendell, Dorothy Thorne and Esme Willey.

A gypsy funeral, Haselbury Plucknett, 1960. Gypsies bought a plot of land at Claycastle in Haselbury in 1930 which, hardly surprisingly, became known as Gypsies Plot. In 1960 the gypsy queen, Eliza Hughes (pictured above right around 1955), who was said to be nearly ninety, died at the site and there were over 120 family mourners at her Yeovil funeral. In accordance with Romany law they returned to Claycastle, burnt her caravan at midnight and shot her horse the following day. The site was later sold and, rather nicely, one of the houses now standing there is called Romnea. The funeral procession, with immaculate Humber, Shearline and Austin Princess vehicles, is seen making its way up out of West Coker between Haselbury and Yeovil.

Haselbury Plucknett Football Club, *c.* 1958. Back row, left to right: -?-, Ted Smith, Howard Randall, Jim Reeves, Basil Williams, Ray Marks, -?-, Mr Harris, Charlie Martin. Front row: -?-, Percy Runciman, Joe Marks, Michael Marks, Alan Brown, Bernard Martin, ? Guppy, Bill Martin.

Swan Hill, Haselbury Plucknett, *c.* 1912. The two Beaumont sisters, Nellie (left) and Gertrude, who lived with their parents at Oak House and were considerable beneficeries to the village in later years, walk down Swan Hill; this takes its name from the Swan Inn, the public house whose sign can be seen at the top on the left. Standing outside his bakehouse on the right is Mr Cooper (with moustache), his daughter Dot and her husband Alfred Champion, who, like the farmer's boy in the song of that name, went to work for the Coopers and ended up marrying the boss's daughter.

Members of Haselbury Plucknett WI, which was founded in 1925 with a membership of fifty, pose with guests outside their new hall at its official opening in 1953. It had been built on land belonging to the Swan Inn and was opened by Mrs W.H. Hebditch, a member of the family firm of that name from Martock who specialized in wooden buildings and were also responsible for the erection of the village hall in 1978.

Sunday school outing, Haselbury Plucknett, c. 1905. The usual destination for this annual outing was 'The Frying Pan', an open space which had been quarried for stone on nearby Ham Hill. It is interesting to see what twenty years has done to the Post Office and Stores in the background. Here it is run by Mr Beaumont, postmaster from 1894 to 1914, and was a grocers and drapers shop. On page 137, when Mr Read had taken over, a handsome entrance and porch has appeared between the shop and post office; previously entry had been by a door at the side. The post office business was transferred to Miss Munro's shop in Swan Hill in 1933.

Clay Castle, Haselbury Plucknett, *c.* 1906.

Pictured centre here in front of his Daimler around 1925 is Jared Geare, a Haselbury Plucknett man who made a fortune in the timber business in London and built four almshouses in the village for the poor and needy at a weekly rental of one shilling. He came back to the village every summer and paid for an outing to the seaside for as many parishioners who wanted to go, giving them all money to spend, oranges for the children and laying on a high tea. The earlier outings were by horse-drawn carriages as far as West Bay near Bridport; later, in the 1920s, the arrival of the charabanc saw the villagers travelling annually to Weymouth.

The earlier Jared Geare outings, such as this one around 1922, always left from outside the Post Office and Stores, the focal point of all village outings. Later the size of the convoy, as seen below, led to the departure point being transferred to Haslebury Cross. Understandably all the people heading off to the seaside with him are wearing happy smiles. Equally understandable, the shopkeeper and his wife(?) with the baby, who do not appear to be having a treat, look rather glum. It would have been as well to have shut up shop for the day, as Haselbury was always a ghost village on Jared Geare's outing day, but the post office regulations forbade this.

Haselbury Cross, *c.* 1928, with a later outing ready for the off. Jared Geare is standing in front of the third vehicle down but the real interest here has to be the fine shot of Pennell King's fourteen-seater charabanc and the larger one in front belonging to Hutchings & Cornelius.

North Street, Haselbury Plucknett, *c.* 1910. Visible at the end of North Street with its outside stone staircase, is the Malthouse, owned by Dunstan Bartlett, a corn merchant who delived by horse and cart over a wide area. It was pulled down to make way for road widening in 1954. The Smithy in front of the malthouse is still standing.

St Michael and All Angels' choir, Haselbury Plucknett, April 1952. Back row, left to right: J. Tilley, C. Paull, K.E. Pinney, E. Lester, A. Mabey, C. Tett, C. Snelgrove, C. Martin. Middle row includes: A. Churchill, F.M. Neal, Revd E.G. Haskins (vicar 1932–52), H.J. Pitt (past churchwarden, a bellringer and for fifty years a chorister who presented this picture to the church), C. Lamb, M. Lester. Front row: F. Tout, T. Marks, K. Snaydon, J. Bryant, B. Durrant, R. Guppy, E. Smith, B. Bromfield.

The Cross, Haselbury Plucknett, *c.* 1920. The thatched cottages on the left have been demolished.

Swan House, Haselbury Plucknett, shortly after its closure as a public house on 5 April 1957. The Swan Inn is thought to have been built at the end of the sixteenth century, and served as a coaching inn at one stage having stables at the end of the building. With its own fields attached, it became popular with drovers who could put their flocks safely away for the night and also find accommodation for themselves. It was partially rebuilt in 1903. Fred Churchill, the landlord from 1920 to 1950, was a cooper by trade and made barrels for many local brewers including Mitchell & Toms at Chard and Crewkerne United Brewery who owned the Swan at one time. His daughter Pamela Rendell took over and still lives there.

St Michael and All Angels' church, Haselbury Plucknett, *c.* 1910. The roof over the lich-gate has been removed, but otherwise the parish church remains largely unaltered. The building on the left, which was behind Oak House and used at one stage as a storeroom, was also thought to have been used as living quarters for the outdoor staff at Oak House. In the 1930s the young men of the village made use of it as a games room, and the Women's Institute also held meetings there. It was later demolished and is now the site of a private house.

Misterton first aid team at Crewkerne station during the First World War. Mr Jeanes is on the extreme right.

Middle Street, Misterton, *c.* 1908. According to the card's caption it was known as Prospect Road at that time. Whatever its name, it was certainly far safer than today when the Dorchester-bound traffic thunders along it.

The post office, Silver Street, Misterton, *c.* 1947. To the left the Miller's Globe (see page 143) has become the plain Globe, grown a second porch but lost both its porch light and the iron railings which went for salvage during the Second World War. Opposite the post office is the blacksmith.

Misterton, *c.* 1905, showing Knowle Cottage at the rear which was pulled down in January 1913 and rebuilt by Mr R.M.P. Parsons. Today the thatched cottage on the right is a garage and filling station.

Misterton School, *c.* 1946.

The Mason's Arms, Silver Street, Misterton, *c.* 1913. Landlord Henry Manley, holding his son Robert in his arms, and his wife pose outside the inn; to his left is Hughie Paull, the village poacher. Manley later moved to the village's other pub, the Miller's Globe (see below), where he was landlord until the early 1950s.

The Miller's Globe Inn, Misterton, *c.* 1925. Henry Manley was the landlord at the time, and it is either his son Harold or Robert in the doorway. Miller was the name of a former landlord but the modern inn has dropped the word from its name.

Misterton Egg Packing Station, *c.* 1950. It closed in the early 1980s, making way for housing development.

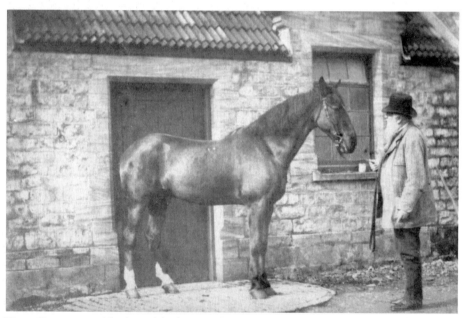

Henry Parsons outside the stable door at Misterton Manor House, *c.* 1890. Parsons, who died in 1895, was the agent for the Portman Estates properties in Somerset and Dorset, the Duke of Devonshire's Somerset estates, Lord Wolviston's Dorset properties, and had several other smaller agencies. In a busy life he also found time to be a director of the Wilts and Dorset Bank, Crewkerne Breweries, *Western Chronicle* Newspapers, and Plymouth Breweries among others. He was also a county councillor, a member of the Chard RDC, and a JP who served as chairman for eleven years on the Crewkerne Bench. In his younger days he played rugby for Somerset.

SECTION SIX

Merriott

The Bell Inn, Merriott, pictured here in 1924 if the Farm Stock Sale poster is as fresh as it looks, was owned by Mr G.T. Symonds who ran a garage and popular vehicle-hire business from the same premises. He used this picture as an advertisement extolling the comfort of his Maxwell 14-seater charabanc (see page 153) as well as a six-seat Chevrolet and a lorry. It seems incongruous to have Shell Oils and 'Fine Old & Mild Beers' vying for attention on the same wall. The Bell, which was an inn as early as 1770, was closed in 1958 and, after being used for a spell as a store by local wholesale stationer Terry Arnold, demolished.

Combined Hinton St George and Merriott Football Clubs who made an Easter Belgian Tour in 1960 at a civic reception at Ostend Town Hall. Among those seen are Derek Pitman, B. Sweet, John Lukins, G. Rawlings, T. Aldridge, K. Alaway, Ron Dash, Micky Pitman, Alwyne Gillard, Ken Chant and M. Haines.

Crewkerne and Hinton St George Red Cross at Hinton House during the First World War. The soldiers are Belgian war-wounded. Miss Lowe, Crewkerne's assistant matron, is centre front next to a soldier; the civilian four from her right is Mr Barlow, headmaster at Merriott School. Also in the picture are three ladies from Merriott, Miss Pamphlet, Miss England (a teacher at Crewkerne's West Street Church School), and Mrs Alice Batstone (a shopkeeper).

Merriott War Weapons Week, *c.* 1942.

Merriott Choral Society, 1910. Among the members posing before a dress rehearsal are, in the back row, Mr Lawrence (second from left), Letty Patten (on his right), and Dick Mitchell (far right). The Revd Stanley Percival, Merriott's rector from 1887 to 1935, sits holding his conductor's baton centre front; behind him and to his right, the England sisters, Bessie the village schoolteacher, and Tressie, sit on either side of 'Old Blind Joe'. Also in the picture are Miss Pamphlet, Mary Mitchell, Herbert Batstone (see page 157), Harry Batstone, and Miss Brake. 'Old Blind Joe' delivered newspapers around the village and, despite his lack of sight, did so without a dog and experienced no difficulty in recognizing the different papers or change.

Alfred Paull, driving the cart below and pictured around 1898 with his wife and family, was the Merriott blacksmith who had his smithy at Broadway. The couple, who are seen on their golden wedding anniversary, were married on 12 August 1890.

Broadway, c. 1912. The cottage with the birdcage on its outside wall (a far from uncommon sight during the nineteenth and early twentieth centuries in the English countryside) is now the car park of Broadway Stores. The nearest cottages on the left have all been renovated considerably; those below went to make way for road widening. Note the muddy state of the road.

Looking up Broadway from The Knapp, c. 1935. Sprake's, now the Acupuncture Supplies, was a gents' hairdresser. Over the years Batstone's shop occupied three different corners at The Knapp. First it was at the bottom corner (see the pictures opposite); in 1921 it moved to where Merriott post office is seen here on the right, and later to the opposite corner just below the car in this picture. In keeping with all this coming and going, Merriott's branch of the Crewkerne & District Co-operative Society moved in 1921 from its site in this picture to the opposite corner (see page 150) taking over from Batstone's.

Looking down Lower Street from The Knapp, *c.* 1910. Jim Pattemore is on the extreme right. Batstone was a draper, in business on the premises until 1921 when the Merriott Co-op took over which is still there to this day.

The Knapp, *c.* 1904. On 4 December 1897 George England fell on the staircase in his tailor and draper's shop on the right behind the cart. He was carrying an oil lamp at the time and the ensuing fire destroyed the shop, the dwelling house, a workshop, and three adjoining cottages. A lot of adjoining thatched properties were endangered but saved by the Crewkerne Fire Brigade (almost certainly many of the men on page six) which 'doused the blaze with a copious stream of water but not before damage estimated at £1,000 was caused'.

Sam Dodge, seen here around 1935, was manager at Court Mill Farm, Merriott for many years.

Workers at Tail Mill, Merriott, *c.* 1922. J. Paull and Henry Farr are holding the horses at the rear. Back row, left to right: George Lawrence, W. Wines, Bobby Lawrence, C. Wines, Ralph and father (Sam) Wills, W. Lawrence, Bert Lawrence. Middle row: Harry Lawrence, P. Wines, Tom Frost, J. Lawrence, Ed Lawrence,Sam Lawrence, Henry Sweet. Front row: A. Lawrence, H. Osborne, J. Ellswood, Jimmy Lawrence, H. Ellswood, W. Hooper, Will Trask, Charlie Trask.

Terry Arnold Ltd, Wholesale Stationers and Printers, set up business at The Knapp in Merriott in the 1930s, and was followed in later years by his son Eric; the firm produced many of the area's postcards, for which it enjoyed a considerable reputation. The business closed in 1986 and the building was converted into housing.

Merriott Football Club 1958, Crewkerne Legion Cup winners. Back row, left to right: Ray Mitchell, Ken Shiner, Arthur Hooper, John Lukins, Derek Osborne, Denny Cossins, Tom Pattemore. Front row: Dave Caddy, Keith Shoemark, the late Aubrey Rowswell (father of snooker professional Brian Rowswell), Brian Lane, Cliff Best. John Lukins, the goalkeeper, was to become probably the best-known personality in local football as sports editor for *Pulmans Weekly News* and its sister paper *The Western Gazette*, both of which give such excellent coverage to all local sport. The former paper was founded in Crewkerne by George Pulman as far back as 1857.

Merriott, *c.* 1927. Pictured outside Church Farm, and looking towards the vicarage, a Sunday school outing is about to set off for an unknown destination. Was it the church's attitude to drink at that time that led them to hire a charabanc from Bird Bros from distant Yeovil rather than local man Mr G.T. Symonds at the Bell Inn?

Charabanc belonging to Mr G.T. Symonds of the Bell Inn, Merriott, *c.* 1925. Pictured prior to setting out on an unknown, all-male occasion, and driven by Symonds's son Jim, are left to right: Jim Symonds, Frank 'Spider' Lawrence, -?-, Charlie Hooper, Henry Lacey, Tom Mitchell, Billy Baker, Arty Gibbs (at back), Ernie Elswood, Harry Mitchell, Joe Marks, Sam Parker, Edward Mitchell.

Merriott School Gardens, *c.* 1920. It is hard to dismiss the thought that the gleaming shovels have been cleaned up especially for the photographer – the boys certainly have. Left to right: G. Sweet, Reg ?, Harry Gibb, Bert Pattemore, Eddie Sprake, Bert Mitchell, Jack Samways, Leonard Swain, George Tett, Ernie Cossins, -?-, Stanley Paul, Bill Hooper, Mr Barlow (the headmaster).

League of Young Patriots, Merriott Council School, *c.* 1917. This is on a similar theme to the picture opposite, but concerned more with the provision of material things rather than simply savings. Among other items, this group has collected 11,560 eggs for local and national hospitals, pretty good going even in a community where almost everyone had a chicken or two scratching around at the end of the garden; 25cwt of apples, the details on the blackboard do not differentiate between apples 'scrumped' and those obtained through more normal channels; twenty-eight sacks of vegetables; and ninety-one walking sticks. The apples and vegetables went to the Fleet, the walking sticks to the wounded.

Infant Class II, Merriott Council School, *c.* 1914. This was the old school now used as the dining-room for the modern school which was built just across the road.

Merriott Council School Savings Association. At the latest this picture could only be mid-1918, probably even earlier, but, since 8 July 1916, eighty children had raised £1,365.0.6d. This was a staggering sum in days when pocket money, if it existed, could be measured in half-pences. Back row, left to right: Mr Barlow (headmaster), S. Lawrence, E. Sprake, Frank Trask, Effie Trask, Evelyn Hooper, -?- (back), Violet Eason, Jean Smith, Joyce Mitchell and George Parker at the back, Minnie Mitchell, May Young, Eliza Clarke-Mitchell (back), Hilda Butcher, Dorothy Hutchings, Annie Osborne (back), Linda Pattemore, Edna Lawrence, Clarice Osborne, Sydney Marks, Vera Marks, Mrs Pamphlett. Front row: Reg Dodge, Arthur Mitchell, Reg Samways, Charlie Trask, Arthur Samways, Sonny Cranton, Bob Mitchell, Willy Butcher, -?-, Mimi Pamphlett, Leonard Paull, Margery Mitchell, Edna Hooper, -?-.

The prefab estates that mushroomed around the country in the wake of the Second World War proved to be a godsend to many a young family. Here, at the Beadon estate in Merriott, Fred and Ruby Bailey and their daughters Rosemary and Hilary stand outside their home around 1955. The modern Lower Beadon council estate was later built here.

Shiremoor Hill, Merriott, *c.* 1903. The houses up this gently rising hill are fine examples of work in Ham stone. Butcher E. Osborne, whose delivery cart is on its round, would have bought much, if not all, of his meat locally and killed it himself.

Although Merriott man Herbert Batstone was working as a baker's roundsman in London when this picture was taken around 1903, he came back first to work as a baker at South Petherton (see page 59) and then back to Merriott where his wife ran a draper's shop. It was impossible to resist the temptation to include it here if only to ask where the bread ended up when he pulled up sharply! Modern generations, raised on cut-bread and other such latter-day 'improvements' in the baking world, may, after sighing at the milk on offer for 4d. a quart (almost two of today's pence) from 'certified healthy cows and sanitary farms', recognize such shapes as split tin, Coburg, bloomer, cob, cottage loaf and barrel among the mountain of bread in the cart. What they would not recognize, unless they have been fortunate to have eaten 'real' bread, is the superb feast on show. Even as late as the end of the nineteenth century the cross on such loaves as the plain round cob, put there to allow the dough to rise more easily, was claimed to 'let the devil out'.

The Kings Head, Church Street, Merriott, *c.* 1901. This lovely old building, which still plays a big part in village life, was built as far back as 1745 and may even have been named in a fit of patriotism when news of Bonnie Prince Charlie's landing reached Merriott – if it ever did! Compare the men's preference here to a gig rather than the governess cart on page 159.

The Mill Pond at Court Mills in 1935. It was filled in around 1961.

Lower Street around 1912. Left to right, Walt Hooper (who worked at Mr Webb's farm) is carrying his milk home, Frank Sweet sits in the cart, and his mother (with the flowers) acted as midwife and laid out people in the village.

Mrs Beatrice White of Ilford House seen outside her home in Lower Street, *c.* 1910. The governess cart was much favoured by the gentler sex because entry was via a rear door rather than a more-dangerous clamber in over the wheel as in a gig or a dog-cart, an important factor with children of course.

Acknowledgements

We are never ceased to be amazed at the trust people, complete strangers in some cases, so often put in us, allowing us to take away their treasured pictures to use. However, old pictures are one of the best ways of getting to know more about the immediate and not-so-immediate past of a community, and those who treasure that past are usually the sort of people who are only too happy to help others share their pictures.

So many have helped, almost invariably giving much of their valuable time to tell us about their pictures, not to mention the occasional and welcome cup of tea, that it would be impossible to thank them all here. But our special thanks must go to Helen Beaufoy, Len Bond, Eric Bowditch, Betty Chant, Derek Cleal, George Cooper, Jeff Farley, Marian Farrow, Robert Gibbs, Ray Harvey, Rodney Hebditch, John Keylock, John Lukins, Vic Matravers, Brian Meecham, Patrick Palmer, Frank Paull, Patricia Pearce, Leslie Parkman, Mollie Rendell, Alan Richards, Cynthia Russell, Valerie Studley, John Stoodley, Charles and Richard Swaffield, Gladys Waterman and John Wills.

In a different direction we must thank our wives, Violet and Jean, for putting up with the disruption to their well-ordered households, the *Chard & Ilminster News* for permission to research certain items in their files, and to Haydon Wood, editor of *Pulmans Weekly News*, for use of a computer in preparing the captions. Without the latter there would have been much burning of midnight oil and copious use of whitener.